TABLE OF CONTENTS

Top Ten Winning Photos by:

Sheldon GOLDSTEIN	4
Nancy ROTENBERG	5
Tom PFEIFER	6
Peter LIK	7
Michael ROSENBAUM	8
James GALLETTO	9
Nancy ROTENBERG	10
Roy TOFT	11
Jeff VANUGA	12
Ron DAY	13
Tier II Images	14
Tier III Images	50
Index of Contributors	80

Front Cover: © *Peter Lik*

All images are wild unless marked captive (Capt) or photo illustrated (Phil).

Expressions, NANPA Showcase 2010
Produced by Loupe Media
Editor: Nicoletta Barrie
Creative Director: Sharon Cohen-Powers

NANPA
North American Nature Photography Association
10200 West 44th Ave., Suite 304
Wheat Ridge, Colorado 80033-2840 USA
303.422.8527, www.nanpa.org

NANPA Showcase Directors:
Wendy Shattil and Bob Rozinski

Published in the United States by Loupe Media (www.loupemedia.com) and NANPA (nanpa.org)

Showcase judges:
Ralph Clevenger, Susan McElhinney, Michele Westmorland

Web support: John Lock / RelevantArts.com

Special thanks to: Susan Day, Bill Jaynes, John Lock, John Nuhn, Annette Rogers, Wendy Shattil

Printed and bound in Canada by Valley Printing & Promotions, 212.655.5784

ISBN 978-1-61658-834-2

Expressions 2010 [illegible] anniversary of *Expressions*, displaying the top 250 images of the annual Showcase competition. Having worked on each of the five editions, I can honestly say that the quality of what has been entered has dramatically improved each year. Where once a simple identification image may have received rave reviews, it is now categorized as commonplace. The subject matter has not changed, for the most part. The plants and animals still have the same physical characteristics, carry on the same behaviors, and survive from day to day, albeit with a little less territory in which to do it. NANPA photographers, however, continue to come up with new twists on the ordinary.

Technology has allowed many situations to be photographed that never could have been captured five years ago, particularly those involving movement and difficult light. To stay ahead of the pack, many now wait for that extra special moment before hitting the shutter button. Low-cost digital capture and processing have given photographers the freedom to make mistakes while trying out new techniques. The results are impressive. Every time we think we've seen it all, we're proven wrong by the creativity of one of our members.

So where do we go from here? Is there a limit to what we'll be able to produce and appreciate? What will change in nature photography during the next five years or even the next twenty? Our three judges, all asked the same question, have varying opinions on this. Michele Westmorland envisions a world that would come to some uniform standards and be technologically superior, where Apple and PC battles would no longer take place, and that one charger would be able to take care of both camera body and battery. She hopes to own a camera system that stays current for longer than 18 months and a small lens that shoots everything from wide angle to telephoto. And she hopes that recycling older gear would be a natural part of the equation.

Ralph Clevenger, on the other hand, thinks that all cameras will be true video capture devices and that still photos will just be a segment frozen from a longer process. But while Ralph believes the files will be larger, he notes that the number and range of the subjects will be much smaller: "The impact of a growing human population coupled with the global crisis in water, arable land and natural disasters will advance the loss of habitat and extinction of many animals and plants alive today." But none of that will matter anyhow, according to Susan McElhinney, because pictures will have less meaning in twenty years than they do today: "I think photography as a medium for capturing the truth and conveying important information will be over because of the abuse of Photoshop and other similar tools. It will not have much relevance anymore."

Me? I'd like to believe that the world will have awakened to the importance of conservation and wildlife...that the planet will make a full recovery from the damage inflicted on it during the last twenty years. And maybe photographers will rediscover the beauty and uniqueness of black and white, which is still my favorite.

—Sharon Cohen-Powers, President

THE ART OF NATURAL SELECTION

by Ethan G. Salwen

"Photography contests are very subjective," explained Michele Westmorland, one of three judges for NANPA's Showcase 2010 competition. "As a judge, I'm going to have my own view, and I'm going to like what I'm going to like." A commercial photographer, Westmorland's personal likes are in line with her passion for underwater and conservation-oriented images. Nonetheless, she is confident that she selected the best of the best during her judging for NANPA's annual contest.

Westmorland spent two days reviewing, rating and narrowing down her selects from the semifinalist images that were presented to her in online galleries by contest organizers. When sharing her process for assessing the work, Westmorland spoke often about the subjective factor. At the same time, however, she stated, "I know what quality is."

"There are some guidelines for judging," said Susan McElhinney, photo editor of *Ranger Rick* magazine and another 2010 contest judge. "But you are bringing your own aesthetics to the process, and different judges will have different final results, which is very interesting." McElhinney shares Westmorland's sentiments that judges can make both completely subjective and totally qualified decisions. "I have a *lot* of experience looking at nature photography," she noted. "And I can quickly see all of the qualities that combine to make an amazing image."

"I have an immediate, gut reaction to great images," Ralph Clevenger explained. A commercial photographer who specializes in nature images and has taught at the Brooks Institute of Photography for 25 years, Clevenger is the third judge of the Showcase 2010 competition. He emphasized that he selected most of the best images "right off the bat" and "almost by intuition." But like his fellow judges—all of whom made their choices independently—Clevenger is confident in his gut reaction as a judging standard.

There are 250 images in *Expressions.* Tier I are the Top Ten winners in the Showcase 2010 competition. Tier II are the next 90 images, which together with the Top Ten will be on the NANPA website throughout 2010. Tier III are an additional 150 worthy images. All were selected with extreme care from the 3,250 submitted to the contest by 387 photographers. Before the three judges got to work, a first cut was made by contest organizers to remove images with general problems. Some 1,000 semifinalist images went to the judges. All judges commented that featuring this scope of images in a printed catalog from a photography contest is unprecedented. The richness of the experience is that the images come from both professionals and amateurs, who go head-to-head with anonymity during judging. The three judges were simply asked to select "the best" in the way they deemed appropriate.

"*Every* image in *Expressions* is great," Clevenger said enthusiastically. "No image is mediocre." Clevenger's strong opinion, although clearly subjective, rings true. Just like the judges, each person who looks through *Expressions* will prefer certain images for greatly different reasons. As McElhinney says, "We all bring our own personal aesthetics to the experience. However, even if we do not respond favorably to a given image, we can see that it has VALUE—both visually and in terms of its content." This is at the heart of what makes the photography in *Expressions* unique: it comprises an inspiring and informative showcase of diverse and excellent nature photography that goes beyond merely a few images in a few categories that are endemic to most photography contests.

"I am always looking for new and interesting photography," McElhinney said of her motivation for serving as a judge. She said that while judging is subjective, there are "objective, quantifiable qualities" that can be found in great images. These include rules of design, use of color, camera techniques and the kind of content that is featured. "Having an image of a coyote standing on its head is not going to get an award unless the light is nice and the image is in focus," she said. "Everything has to work, although priorities are not the same in every image."

"In judging what's best, I do think you have to look at an animal behavior shot differently than a landscape," Clevenger said about this concept of priorities. "In an image with two lions fighting what's important is the focus, the position of the claws, the decisive moment. Landscape is all about light and composition, waiting for perfect light, which is capturing another kind of decisive moment." Clevenger explained that in his judging process the best macro thumbnails shouted out to him even before he looked at their enlargements. Not so with landscapes, where he carefully studied the visual subtleties in the larger view before making judgments.

Westmorland made the point that judges access images differently based on their own photographic specialty. "Because I am an underwater photographer, I have the ability to identify an underwater image that is particularly hard to create," she explained. But while her specialty affects her experience of judging—her appreciation as a viewer—Westmorland made it clear that experienced professionals can judge outside their own specialties. This idea points to the importance of selecting three judges with broad experience. Clevenger brings to the process his two decades helping students compare their work to pros. McElhinney brings her perspective as a leading picture editor in nature imagery. Diverse, critical eyes bring quality to the judging process.

Clevenger noted that his critical eye changes from one context to another, such as whether he is critiquing lower division students versus upper division students or whether he is judging a photography contest for a commercial publication with large cash prizes or one with no prizes at all. "What is the best photograph?" he posited. "With the upper division students I am comparing their images to the work in the commercial industry, and so I provide feedback in terms of marketability. Commercial photography is about solving a problem. Showcase 2010 is about presenting the best nature photography. With this contest, I realized I was looking at pros and amateurs and for simply what is the best, and so I was looking for visual impact." Clevenger said that he looked for what made him go "Wow!"

All of the judges spoke of the freedom of creativity the contest encourages. They suggested that future participants embrace the opportunity to push themselves creatively and reach out to the wider community in a non-commercial framework. However, McElhinney cautioned photographers not to do any "extreme stuff" in Photoshop. "Some people are making a mistake about what they think photography is," she said. "I think they need to remember what the fundamentals are. Photography is about capturing something in camera, a moment, using light."

McElhinney believes many professionals get into creative ruts, falling back on safe techniques that go stale. "Mimic what other people do," she suggests to pros and amateurs alike, noting that producing creatively fresh work is usually about subtle shifts in approach, not massive departures. "Just when I think I can't stomach another hummingbird image, one comes in that is totally fresh," she said. "There is always the opportunity for photographers to do something familiar, but in their own style."

Ultimately, perhaps how or why photography contest judges select the images they do is not important. As McElhinney said, "To have the most successful contest experience, I think photographers just have to be themselves. Too many people are trying to figure out what the judge wants. But they need to just say, 'This is my vision.'"

Ethan G. Salwen is a writer and photographer based in Buenos Aires, Argentina.

★TIER 1

WINNER

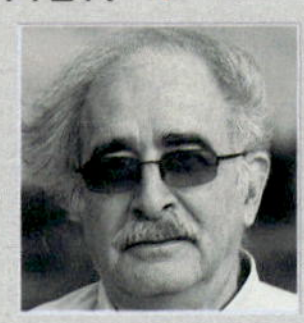
©Sheldon Goldstein

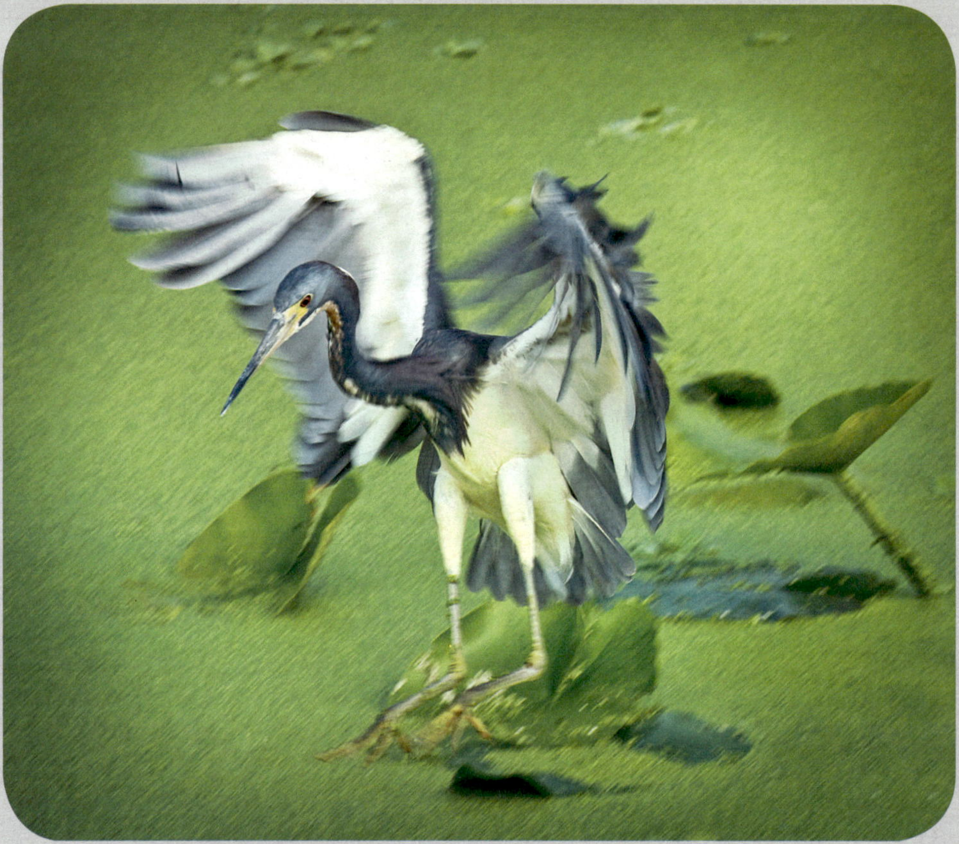

Coming in for a Landing

© Sheldon GOLDSTEIN

SHELDON GOLDSTEIN takes daily walks close to home at Green Cay and Wakodahatchee Wetlands in Delray Beach, Florida. He always takes a camera with him and stops along the way to take pictures. On a day in July 2009, Shelly saw this heron landing. "I didn't have a chance to check my settings," he says, "I just took a burst of shots." He feels this one works because the body of the heron was still, while the movement in the wings caused an interesting motion blur.

Shelly used a Canon EOS-1D Mark III, 100-400mm lens at 320mm, ISO 400, f/18 at 1/160 sec.

Shelly is a lawyer by profession and a nature photographer by preference. He became interested in photography as a teenager, and his interest turned into an obsession with the advent of the digital SLR. Shelly's photographic interests are landscape and nature—primarily avian photography. He was commended by NANPA with second and third place honors in the 2007 Fine Art Exhibit Awards in the Fauna category. His predilection is photographing birds as part of the landscape as well as capturing bird behavior. To see more of Shelly's work, go to www.shellysphotoart.com.

"I was in St. Augustine, Florida, for bird photography," says **NANCY ROTENBERG,** "but there are always unexpected surprises if you're willing to be open to the gifts." She took advantage of the soft, ethereal light of an early morning sunrise to photograph a starfish in the surf in March 2009.

Nancy used a Nikon D3, 24-70mm lens and tried many images, hoping for the timing of the sunrise light connecting with the wave.

Nancy is an award-winning photographer, feature writer and educator. Her two new books, *Photography and the Creative Life* and *La Luz del Pueblo, Discovering a Sense of Place in San Miguel, Mexico*, and her two-part DVD, *Let Your Light Shine*, form the foundation for her photographic philosophy and emphasis on the creative aspects of art and life. Nancy is a popular motivational speaker, leading workshops and seminars throughout the world. To see more of Nancy's work, go to www.naturaltapestries.com, www.animalsanimals.com or the Jaynes Gallery at www.danitadelimont.com.

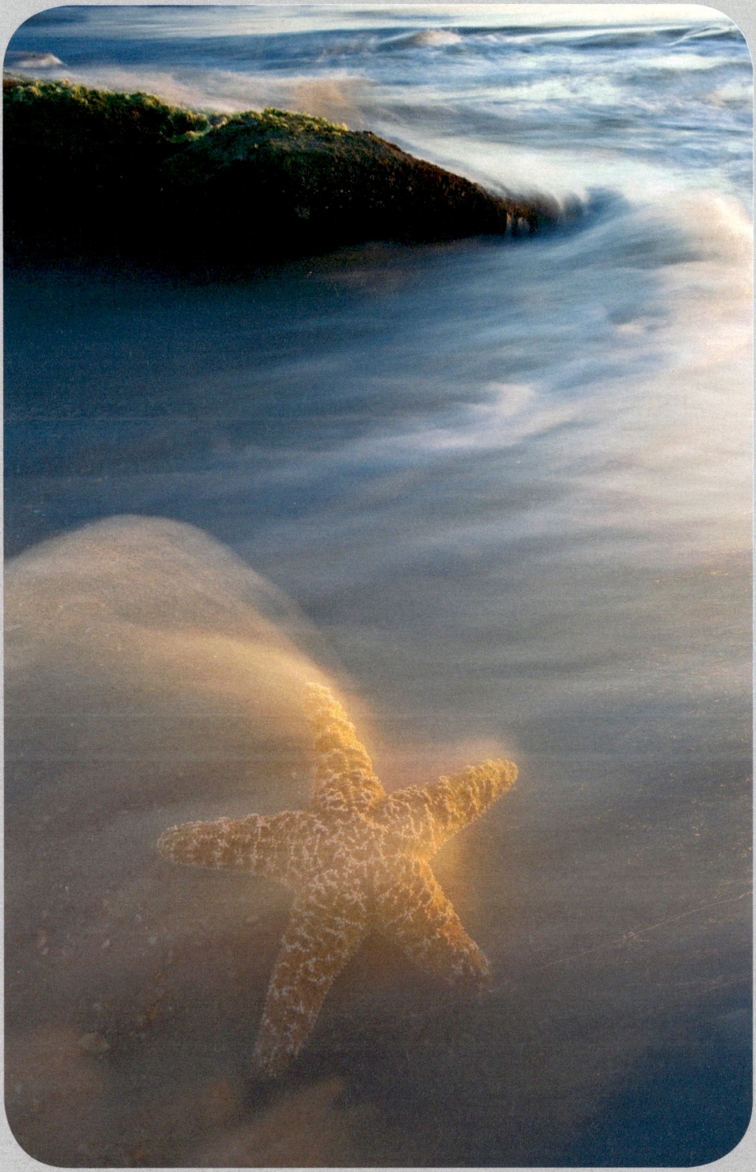

SUNRISE STARFISH
© Nancy ROTENBERG

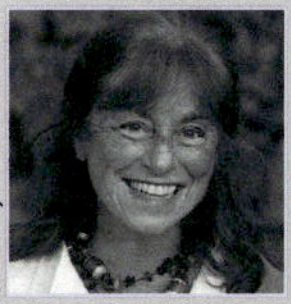

©Jeremy Woodhouse

WINNER

TIER 1 ★

★TIER 1

WINNER

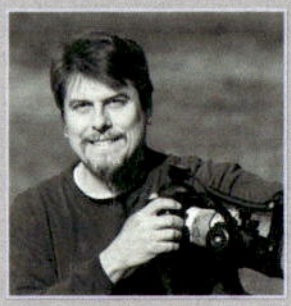

©Emily Pfeifer

TOM PFEIFER had been trying to capture a pleasing image of slugs mating for some time. "Most often, the snails are found slithering close to the ground," he says. "But they make a vertical climb in August and descend together to mate in midair." The challenge was to set up and take the shot of the constantly moving pair before the short-lived ballet was over. In August 2009, Tom found success by photographing this pair dangling from a tree in the dark near his home in East Northport, Long Island, New York.

Tom used a Canon EOS 20D, 24-70mm f/2.8L lens, 580EX flash and a tripod, ISO 400, f/4 at 1/60 sec.

Tom spends much of his time photographing local wildlife around his home on Long Island. "Each season presents us with an abundant assortment of wildlife and holds its own unique definition of beauty," he says. Tom hopes his images stimulate an awareness of the beauty and diversity of Long Island's natural environment and help to foster a widespread interest in protecting and preserving the integrity of our landscape and its inhabitants. To see more of Tom's work, go to www.naturalvisionsimaging.com.

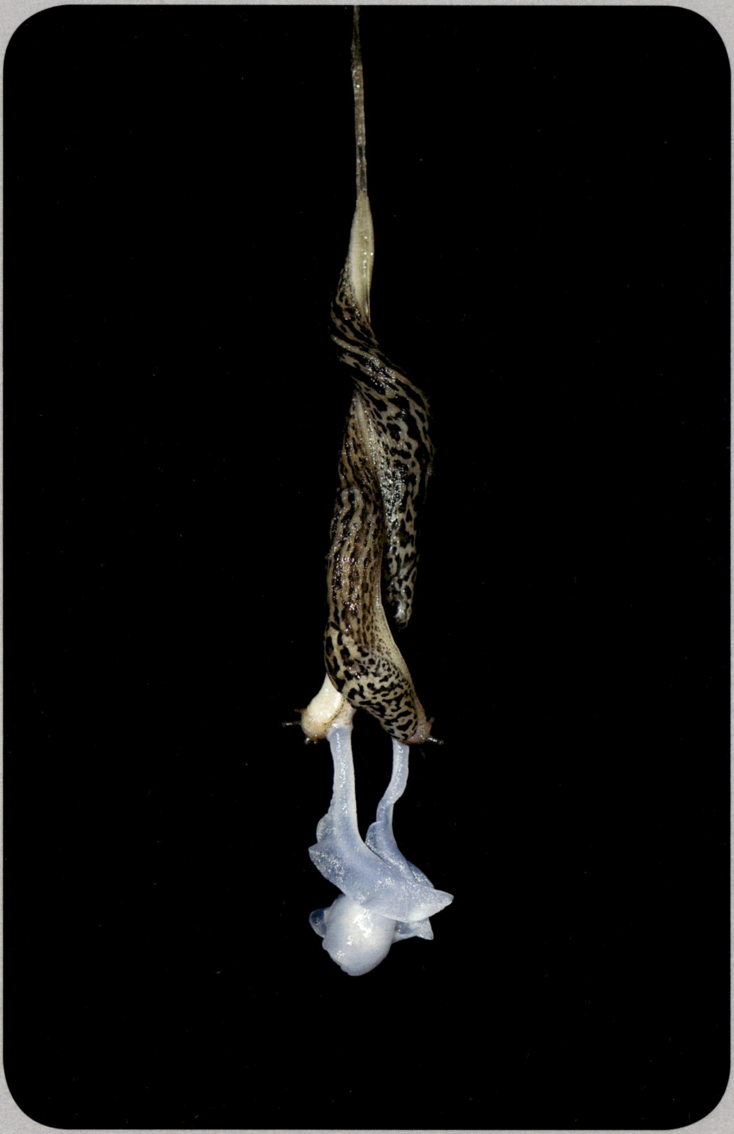

Slugs in Love

© Thomas PFEIFER

PELE'S WHISPER

© Peter LIK

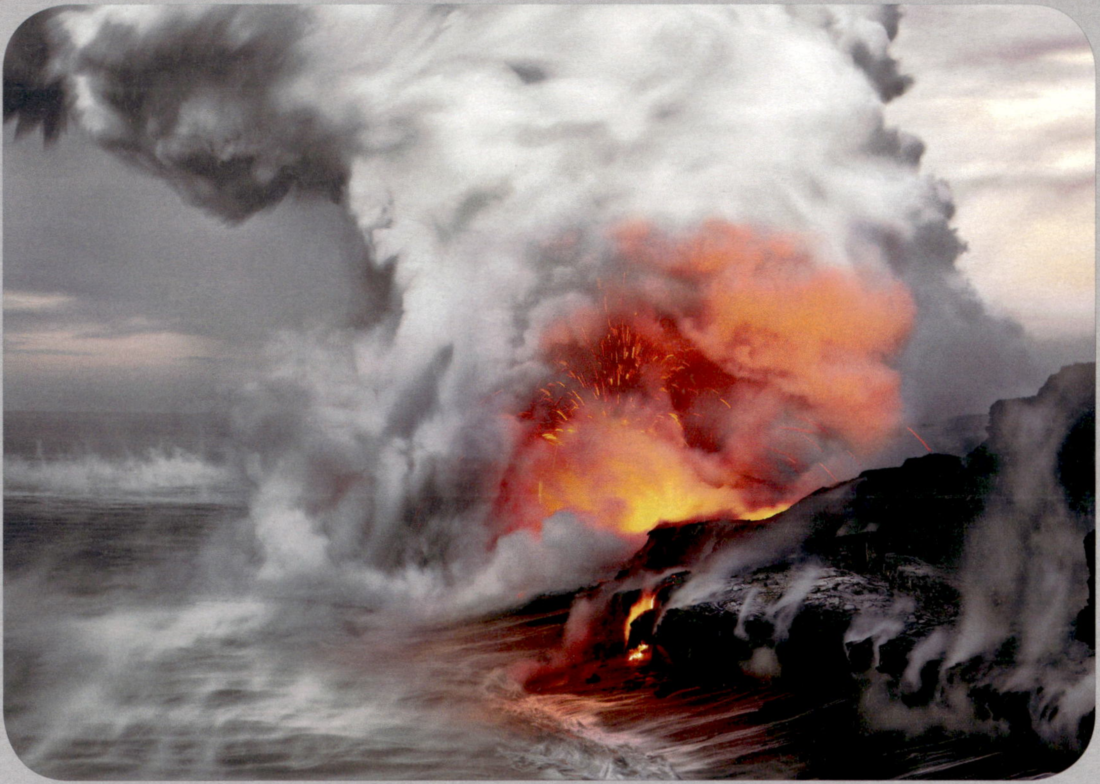

"As I hiked out under moonlight over the smoldering crunchy lava," says **PETER LIK** about his September 2008 trip to the Kilauea Volcano, Kalapana, the Big Island, Hawaii, "an eerie electricity filled the air and I couldn't help but think that something momentous was in store." Later a friend told Peter the story of Pele, the Goddess of Fire in Hawaiian folklore. A volatile and, at times, vindictive goddess, Pele took pleasure in her power to both destroy the land and also create it. Legend has it that she and her sister Na-maka-o-Kaha'i, Goddess of Water and Sea, constantly sabotaged each other causing Pele to move down the island chain before finally claiming the Mauna Loa Mountain on the Big Island. "You can visualize her fair profile in the upper left," continues Peter. "It is like she is blowing or whispering into the ocean, causing the steam to part on the surface. I get chills every time I look at it. It's my shot of a lifetime."

Peter used a Hasselblad H2, 50mm lens and tripod, f/11 at 2 sec.

Born in Australia, self-taught landscape photographer Peter Lik grew up within the confines of Melbourne's "urban jungle," which nurtured his respect and reverence for the wide-open spaces of the Australian landscape. He is an accredited Master of Photography by the Australian Institute of Professional Photography (AIPP). For more than 30 years, Peter honed his craft. He was prolific and experimental, pushing the boundaries of traditional photographic techniques. Peter has a respect for the power of nature, a connection with the land, and a commitment to preserving the "spirit of place" in his images. Although a successful businessman, Peter remains more comfortable behind the lens of his camera than behind a desk and spends much of his time traveling. To see more of Peter's work, go to www.peterlik.com.

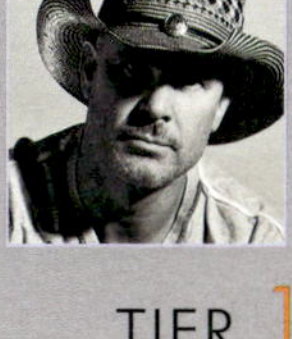

©Michael Plumridge

WINNER

TIER 1 ★

★ TIER 1

WINNER

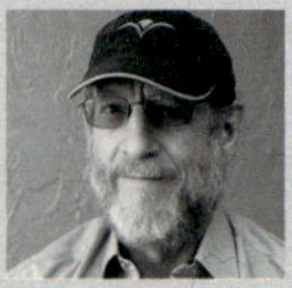

©Barbara Miller

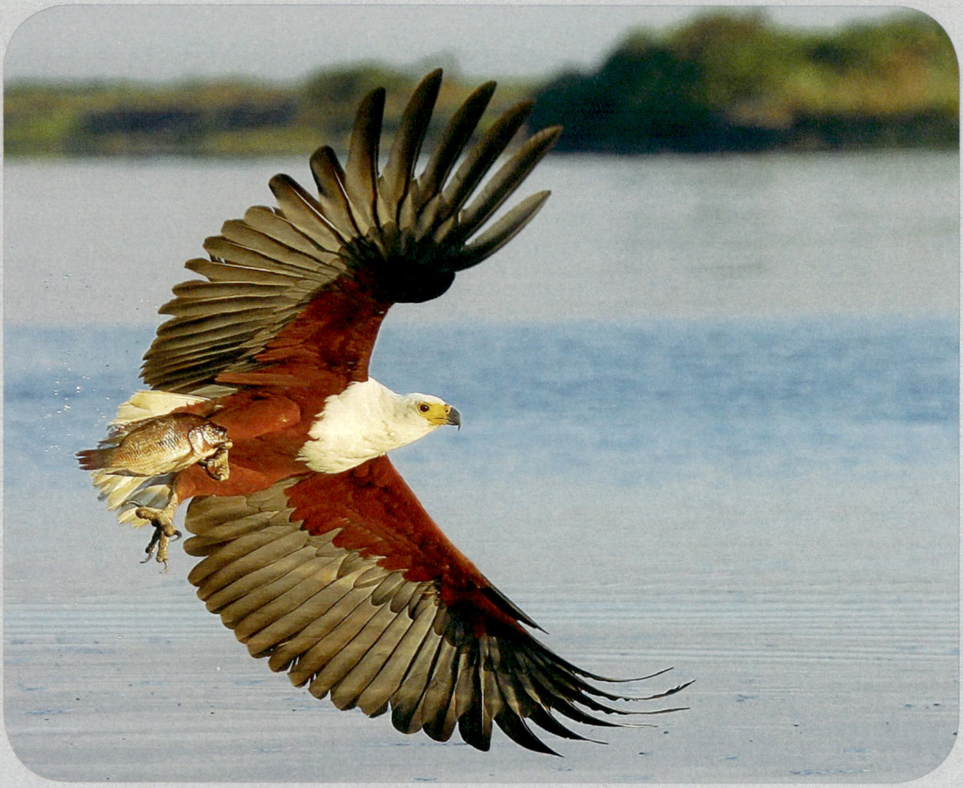

Fish Eagle with Fish

© Michael ROSENBAUM

The Chobe River in Botswana is frequented by hippos, antelope, elephants, other mammals, reptiles and some species of birds, including fish eagles. On a trip to Botswana in 2008, **MICHAEL ROSENBAUM** took a boat out on the Chobe River several mornings in succession to take photographs. On the last morning, he captured this fish eagle making a catch.

Michael shot in the manual mode and used a Canon EOS-1D Mark III and a 100-400mm lens.

Michael purchased his first SLR camera in 2006 after becoming involved in environmental protection groups and spending time birdwatching. He says his mission is "documenting bird behavior as well as portraying wildlife in behavior that is interesting or aesthetically pleasing." Michael also teaches action photography locally. To see more of Michael's work, go to www.flickr.com/photos/michael_rosenbaum.

Grace in Flight

© James GALLETTO

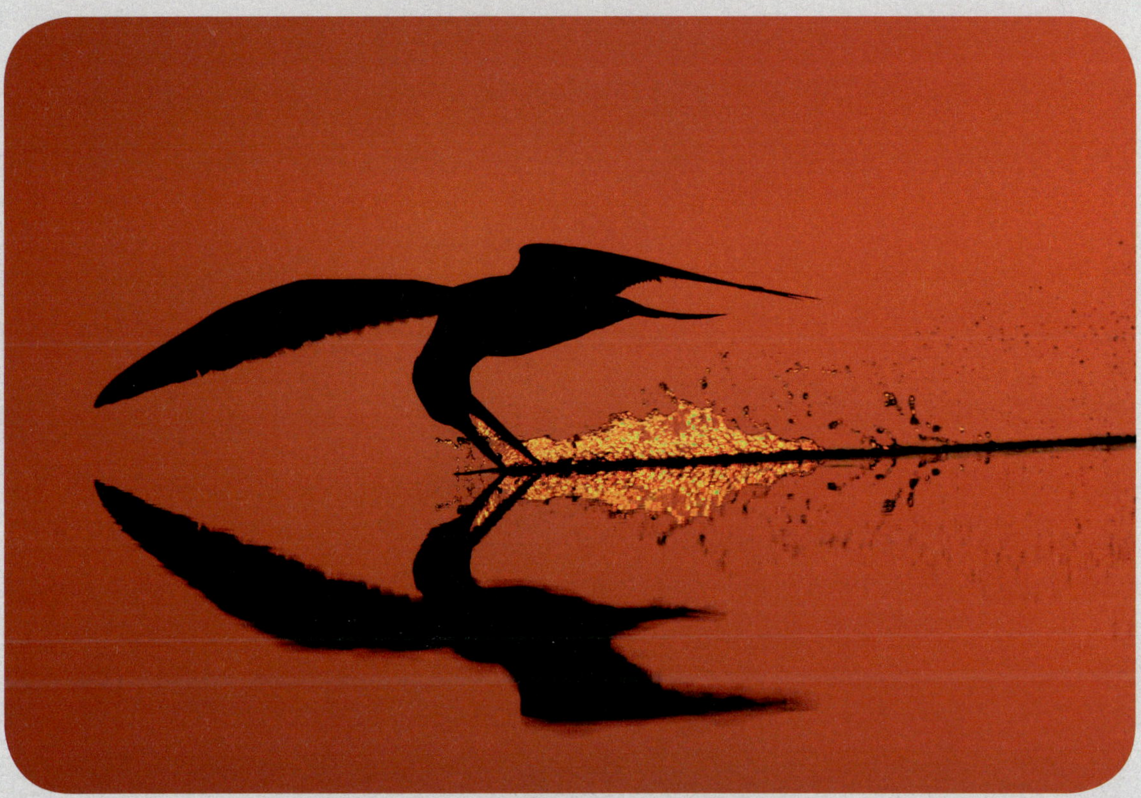

Following a weather forecast for calm winds at Nickerson Beach in Nassau County, New York, **JAMES GALLETTO** decided to get out there early to photograph. Once he arrived, he noticed the wonderful warm glow of the sunrise reflecting in the standing puddles from a recent flood. As a skimmer gracefully dipped its bill in the water to take a drink, James snapped the bird in motion.

James used a Canon EOS-1Ds Mark III, 500mm f/4 lens, 1.4x extender, ISO 400, f/5.6 at 1/1600 sec.

James has been photographing nature for ten years, and his passion is in capturing animal behavior and the daily lives of his subjects. James's mentor is Charles Glatzer, whom he credits with "making me the photographer I am." To see more of James's work, go to www.jimmygsnaturephotos.homestead.com/Jims.html.

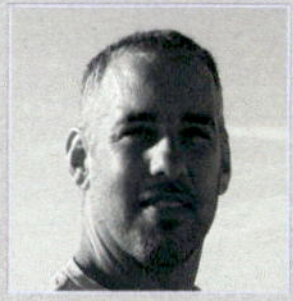

©Tyler Such

WINNER

TIER 1 ★

★TIER 1

WINNER

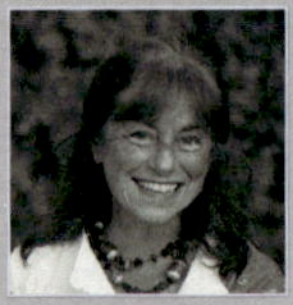

©Jeremy Woodhouse

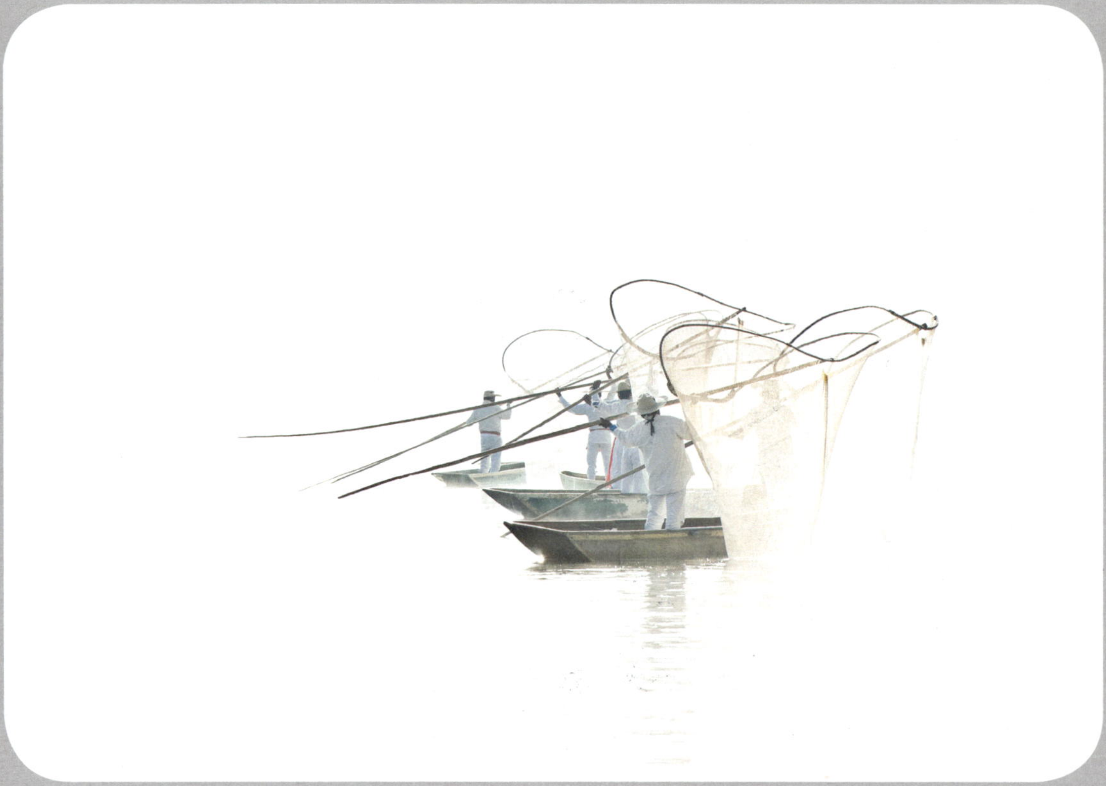

Butterfly Fisherman

© Nancy ROTENBERG

Indigenous fishermen in Mexico lower their butterfly-shaped nets to catch "pescado blanco" (local cold-water white fish) in Lake Pátzcuaro, Michoacán, on an early morning in January 2009. Modern fishermen do not bother with this artful "dance" of the butterfly fishermen whose numbers are declining but whose graceful yet strenuous practice resembles a waltz.

NANCY ROTENBERG used a Nikon D3, 70-200mm lens and overexposed in the fog conditions to create a "high-key" moody impression.

Nancy is an award-winning photographer, feature writer and educator. Her two new books, *Photography and the Creative Life* and *La Luz del Pueblo, Discovering a Sense of Place in San Miguel, Mexico*, and her two-part DVD, *Let Your Light Shine*, form the foundation for her photographic philosophy and emphasis on the creative aspects of art and life. Nancy is a popular motivational speaker, leading workshops and seminars throughout the world. To see more of Nancy's work, go to www.naturaltapestries.com, www.animalsanimals.com or the Jaynes Gallery at www.danitadelimont.com.

While photographing a bald eagle returning to its nest on the pristine cliffs of the Alaskan Katmai coast, **ROY TOFT** witnessed a black oystercatcher parent mobbing the eagle. The oystercatcher's nest was on the beach below the cliff, and whenever the eagles returned to the nest, they were met with "screeching mach-five dive bombs," says Roy, who captured this image in June 2009. Roy used a Canon EOS-1D Mark III, EF 600mm f/4L IS USM lens, f/7.1 at 1/800 sec.

An award-winning photographer, Roy is dedicated to documenting the natural world for future generations, focusing on wild images that convey a sense of the animal's character and spirit. His images have been featured in *National Geographic, Nature's Best Photography, Smithsonian, Audubon, Wildlife Conservation* and *Discover* magazines to advance conservation efforts globally. He is a founding fellow of the International League of Conservation Photographers (ILCP). Roy's company, Toft Photo Safaris & Gallery, sponsors annual workshops for photographers to destinations that include Costa Rica, Japan, Alaska and Africa. To see more of Roy's work, go to www.toftphoto.com.

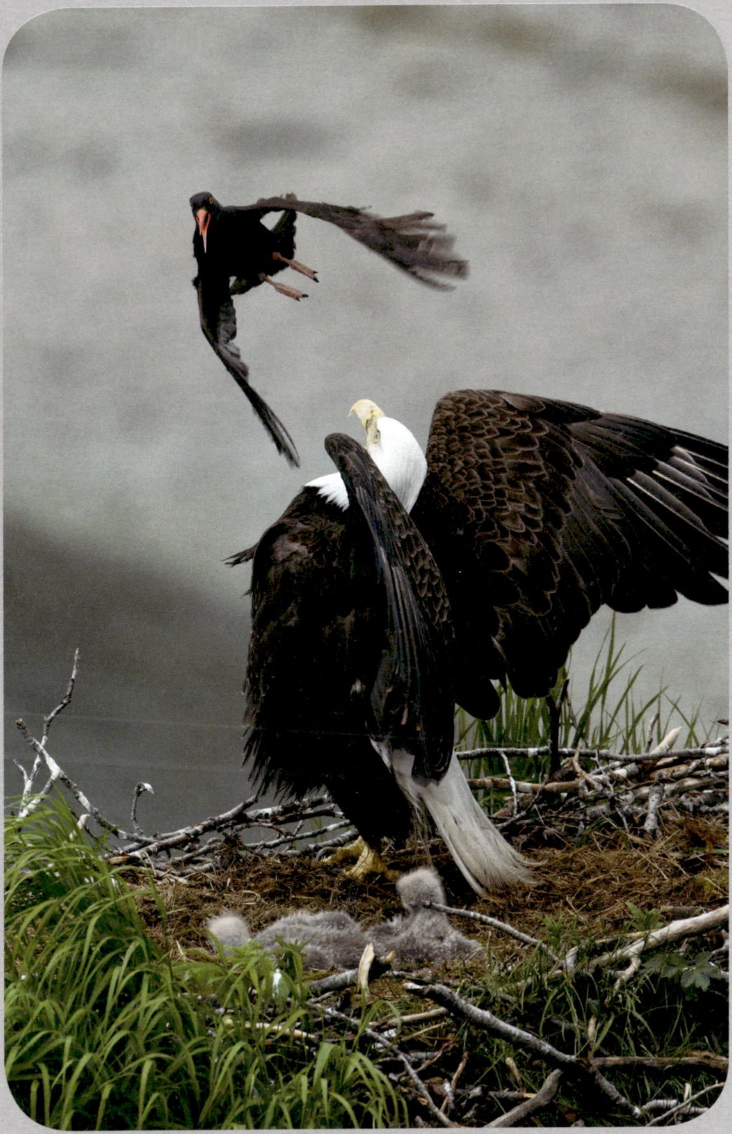

PARENTAL VIGILANCE

© Roy TOFT

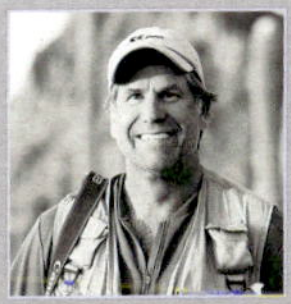

©Kevin Schafer

WINNER

TIER 1 ★

★ TIER 1

WINNER

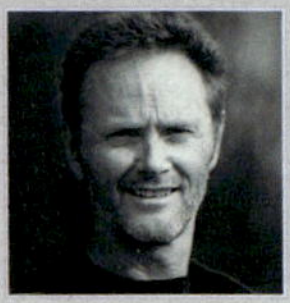

©Anna Vanuga

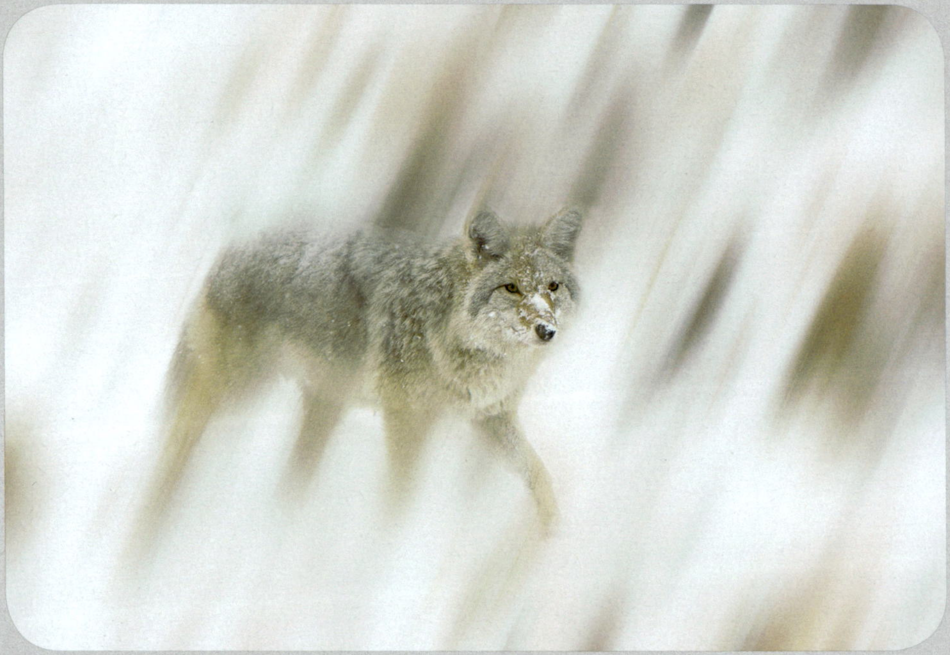

Yellowstone Coyote

© Jeff VANUGA

JEFF VANUGA was with another photographer near Mud Volcano in Yellowstone National Park, Wyoming, in October 2008 when he noticed this coyote. "I was hoping to capture the coyote jumping as it was hunting through the meadow," says Jeff. "There was nothing special about the situation, especially since the light was poor and the barren ground had mixed snow." But back in the office, Jeff worked on the image in Photoshop to give it more artistic expression. It has since become one of his best-selling prints.

Jeff used a Canon EOS-1D Mark III, 70-200mm f/2.8 L lens with 1.4x extender, ISO 320, f/7.1 at 1/1000 sec.

Jeff is a widely published photographer who has shot professionally for the last 30 years. His work has been featured in magazines, advertising, books and calendars worldwide. Jeff leads workshops for Joseph Van Os Photo Safaris. To see more of Jeff's work, go to www.jeffvanugaphotography.com, www.corbis.com, www.naturepl.com and www.agpix.com.

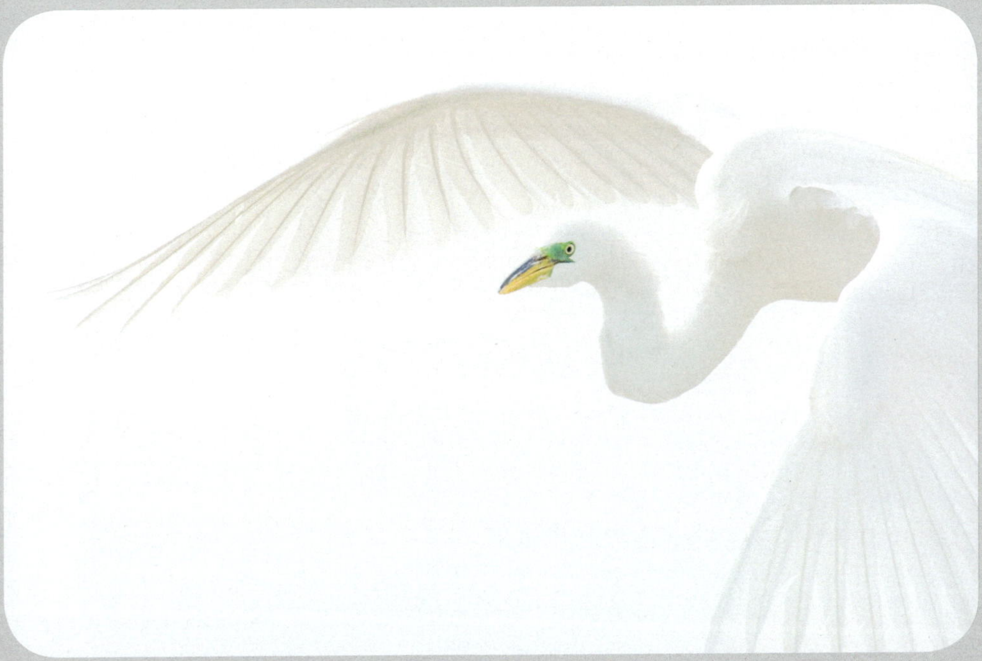

Great Egret in Breeding Plumage

© Ron DAY

RON DAY left home at 4 a.m. in the rain on May 4, 2009, to photograph fox kits. When he arrived at Grand Lake in northeast Oklahoma, however, the weather was still rainy and there was not a kit to be found. Just as it looked as though the day would be a wash, another photographer tipped off Ron about some great egrets near the water. As the rain gave way to light fog and an overcast sky, Ron selected a long lens with the intent of capturing a great egret in flight, revealing the lime green lores of its breeding plumage. The light tones in both the sky and the egret proved ideal for this high-key rendition. "Although using a long glass on a large bird in flight at relatively close range pushed me outside of my comfort zone," says Ron, "I was able to create an image which otherwise would not have been possible."

Ron used a Nikon D2Xs, 500 mm f/4 lens, 1.7x teleconverter and tripod, ISO 400, f/8 at 1/2000 sec.

Ron has been photographing nature and wildlife for more than 15 years. He puts the same planning and hard work that went into building a successful law practice into his photography. Ron's images have been published in *National Wildlife, Nature's Best Photography, Nature Photographer, Peterson's PHOTO-graphic, Outdoor Oklahoma, Boating Life, Equus, Wild Bird,* and *Birder's World* online. To see more of Ron's work, go to www.rondayphotography.com.

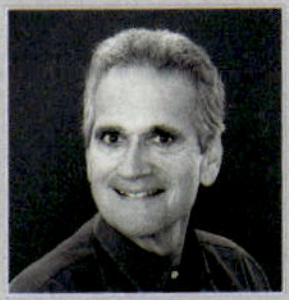

©M. Waldroop

WINNER

TIER 1 ★

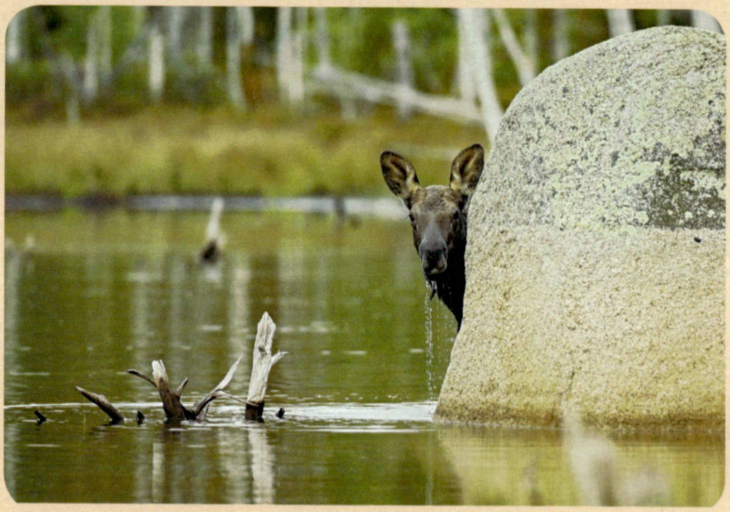

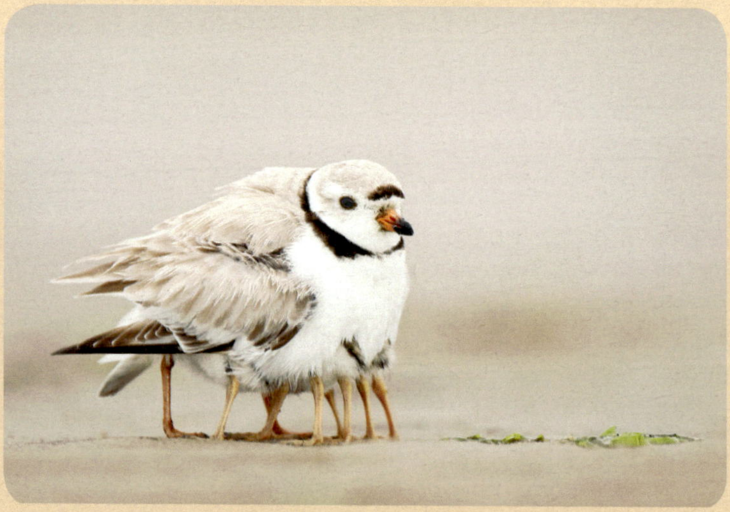

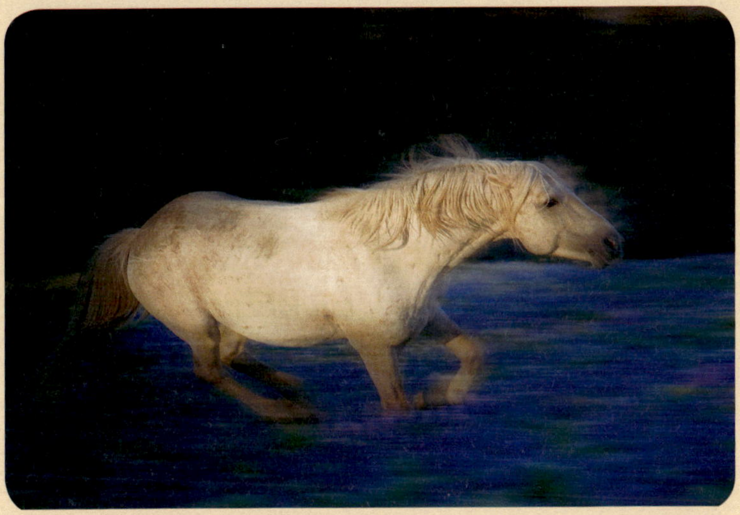

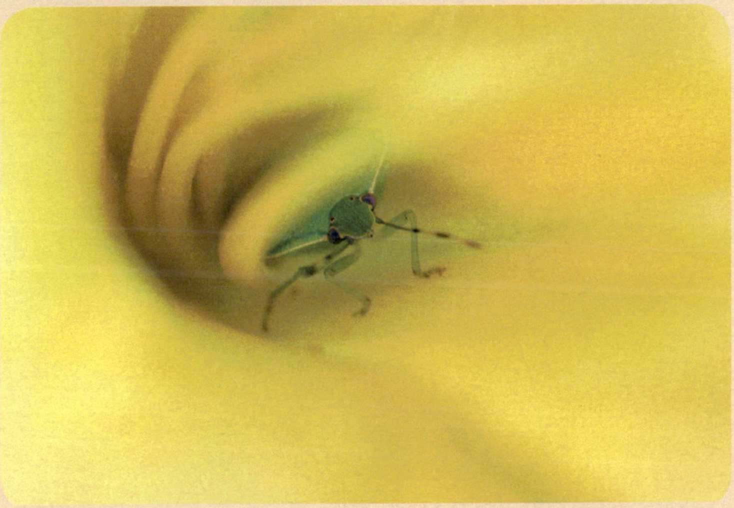

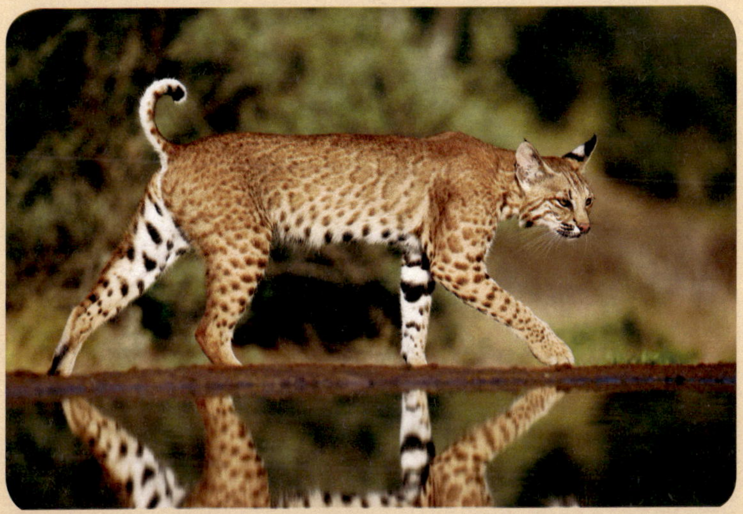

LEFT

Top:
Moose Calf Behind Glacial Boulder, Baxter State Park, Maine, *©George Sanker*

Bottom:
Piping Plovers, Plum Island, Massachusetts, *©Michael Milicia / Michael Milicia Photography*

RIGHT

Top:
Cloud, Stallion of the Pryor Mountains, Wyoming, *©Jeff Vanuga / Vanuga Photography*

Middle:
Shield Bug in Flower, Western Pennsylvania, *©Nancy Rotenberg / Natural Tapestries*

Bottom:
Female Bobcat, Santa Clara Ranch, South Texas, *©Jeremy Woodhouse / PixelChrome, Inc.*

HIDE N' SEEK

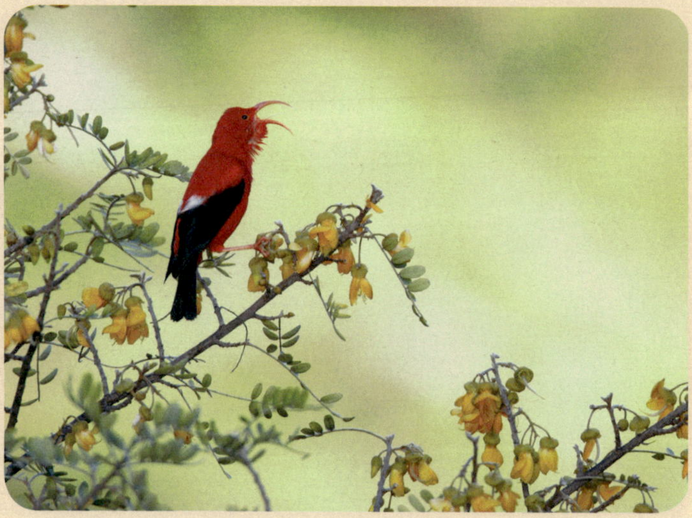

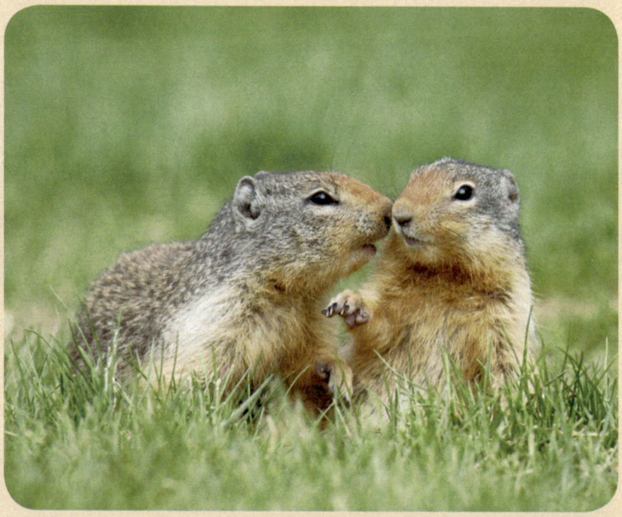

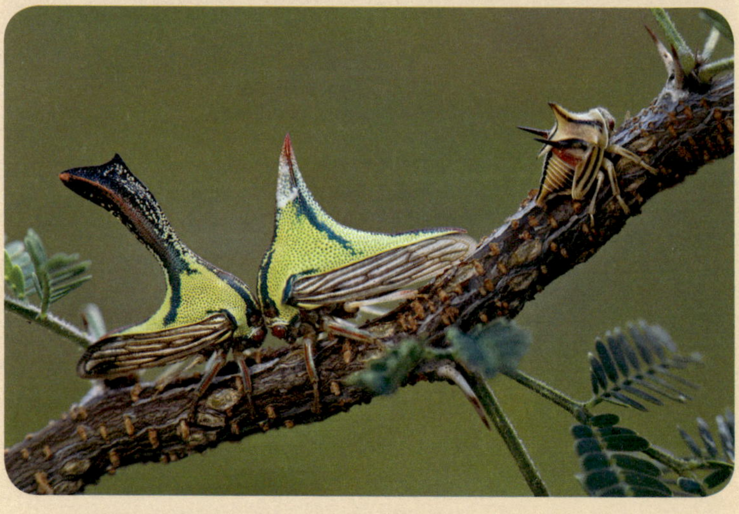

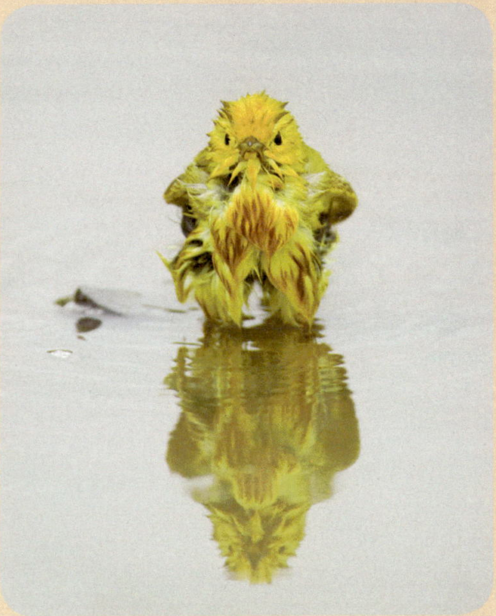

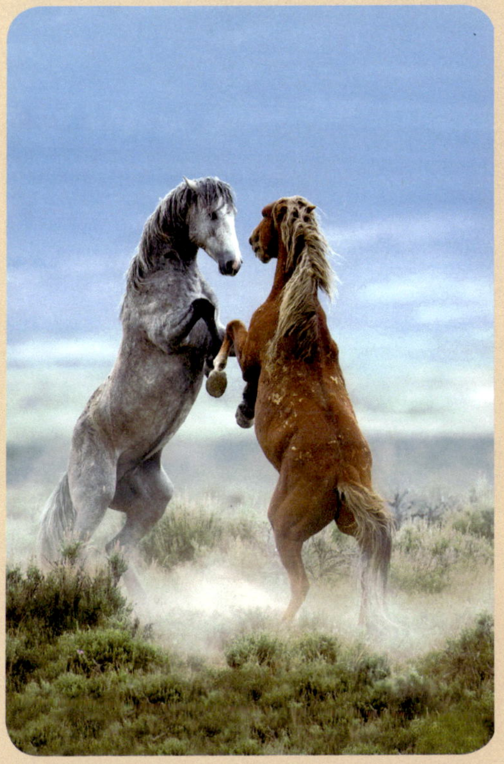

LEFT

Top:
Singing I'iwi in Mamane, Haleakala National Park, Maui, Hawaii, *©Jack Jeffrey / Jack Jeffrey Photography*

Middle:
Columbian Ground Squirrels, E.C. Manning Provincial Park, British Columbia, Canada, *©Jan Forseth / ImagesOfColorado.com*

Bottom:
Thornbugs on Sweet Acacia, Largo, Florida (Phil), *©Christina Evans / ChromaGraphics Studios, Inc.*

RIGHT

Top:
Yellow Warbler, Great Swamp National Wildlife Refuge, New Jersey, *©Jim Gilbert*

Bottom:
Fighting Wild Stallions, Bureau of Land Management Land, Wyoming, *©Irwin Glazer / Glazer Creative Group*

COMMUNICATE

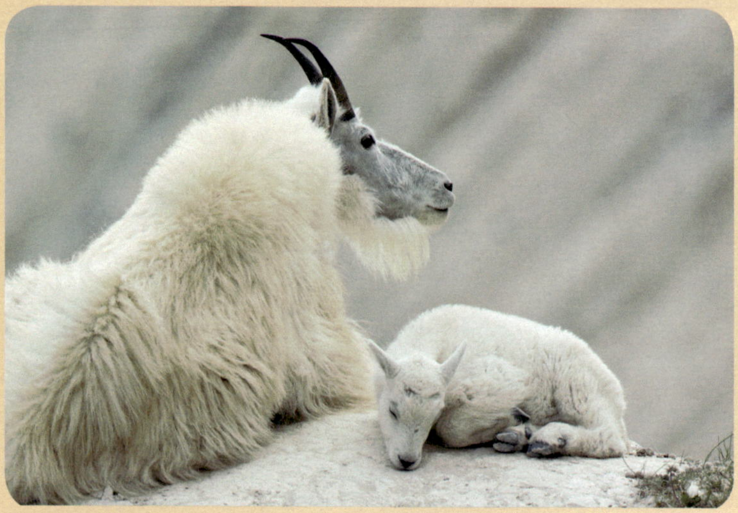

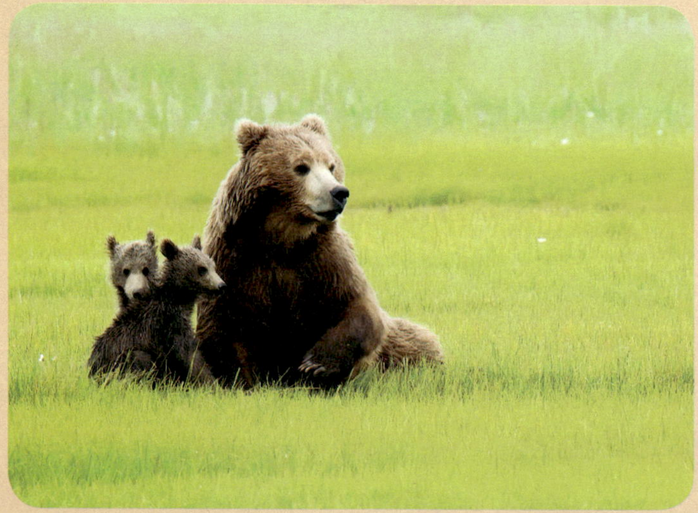

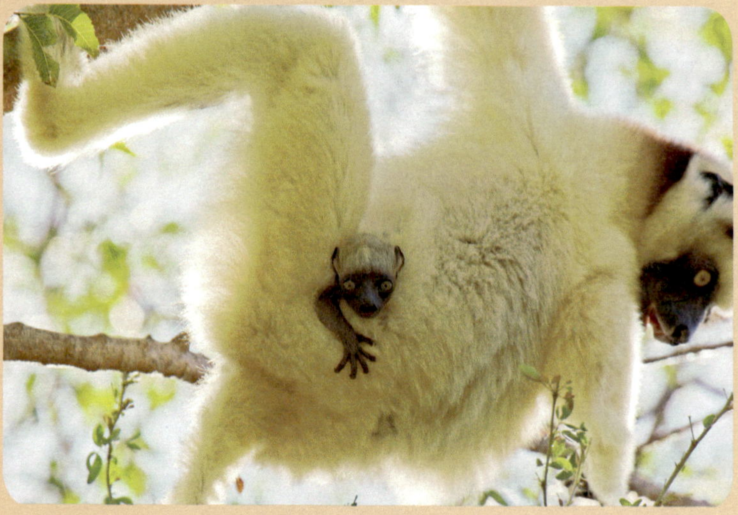

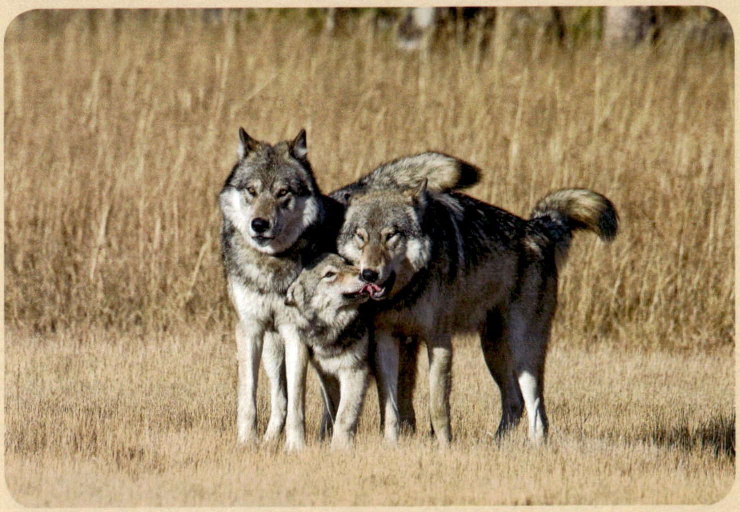

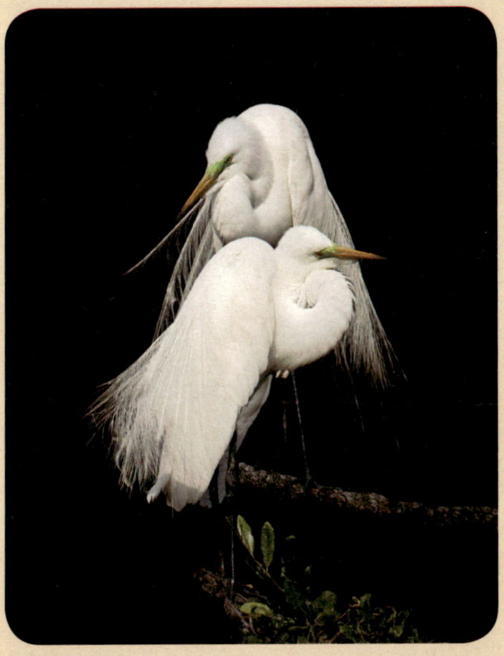

LEFT

Top:
Mountain Goat Nanny and Kid, Jasper National Park, Alberta, Canada, ©*Roberta Olenick / Never Spook the Animals Wildlife Photography*

Middle:
Mother Grizzly with Cubs, Hollow Bay, Katmai, Alaska, ©*Judith Malloch*

Bottom:
Verreaux's Sifaka Lemurs, Madagascar, Africa, ©*Steve Mandel*

RIGHT

Top:
Gray Wolves, Yellowstone National Park, Wyoming, ©*Kim Hart / Kim Hart Wildlife Photography*

Bottom:
Great Egret Breeding Pair, St. Augustine, Florida, ©*Shawn Marques / Shoot To Thrill Images*

PROTECT

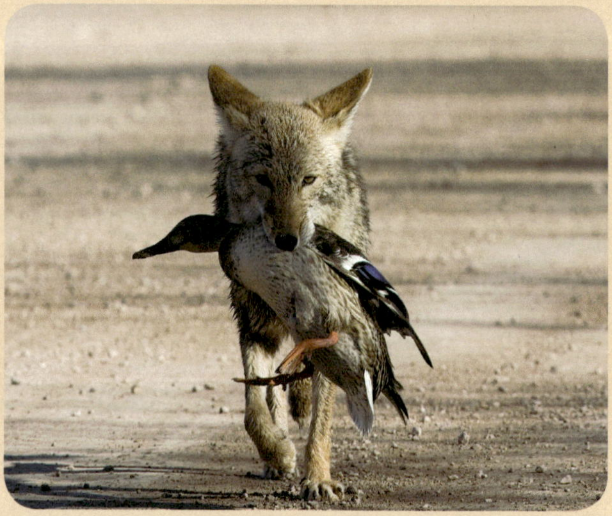

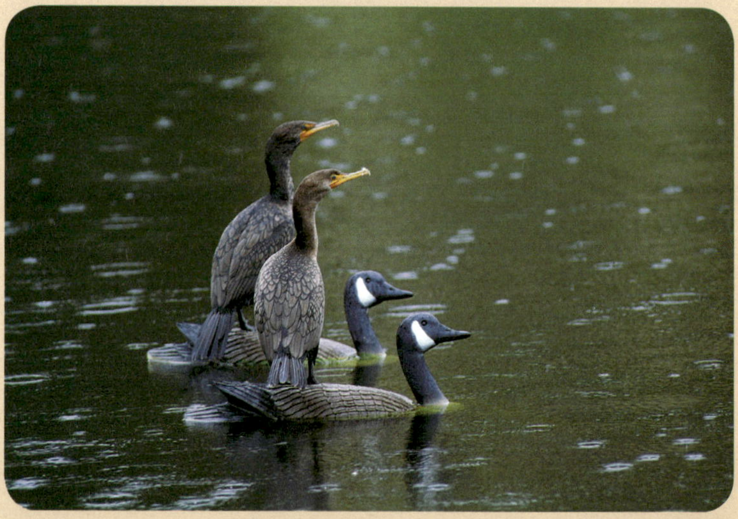

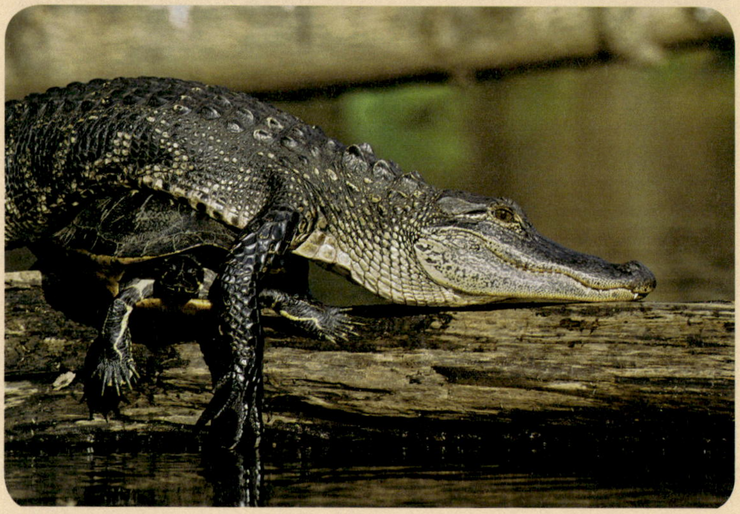

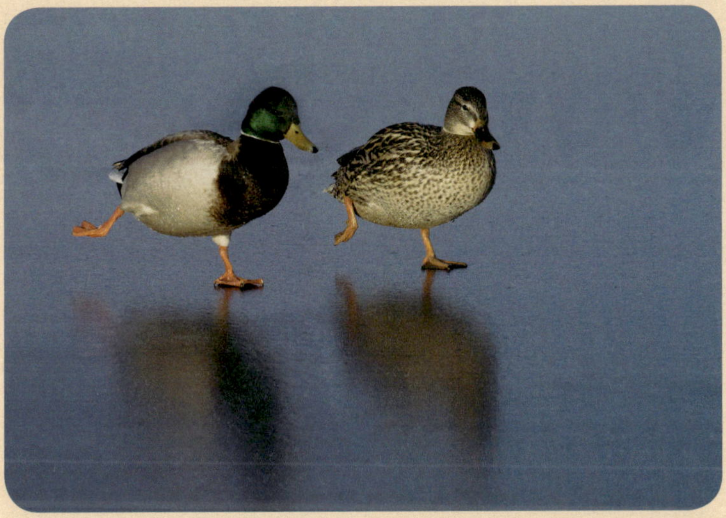

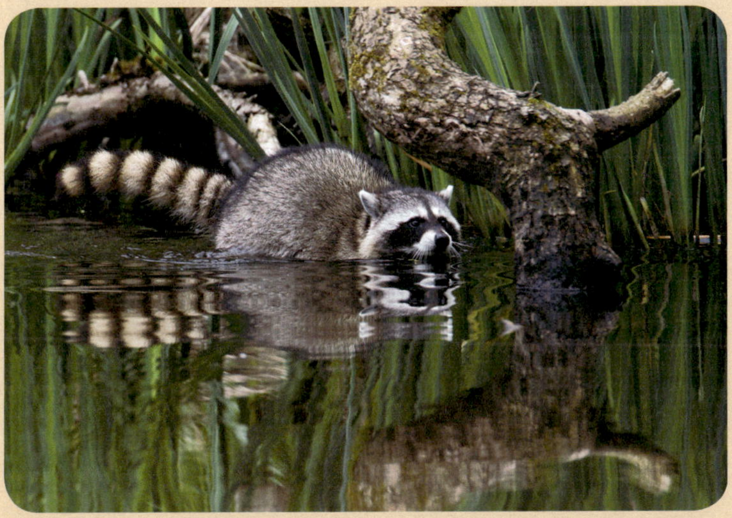

LEFT

Top:
Coyote with Next Meal, Bosque del Apache National Wildlife Refuge, New Mexico, *©Diane Johnson / Diane Johnson Photography*

Middle:
Cormorants on Decoys in Rain, Florida, *©Nancy Rotenberg / Natural Tapestries*

Bottom:
Alligator Climbing over Red-bellied Turtle, Hillsborough River, Florida, *©George Sanker*

RIGHT

Top:
Ice Dancing Mallard Pair, Kettring Park, Littleton, Colorado (Phil), *©Lara Hardesty / Lara Hardesty Nature Images*

Bottom:
Raccoon Wading, Stanley Park, Vancouver, British Columbia, Canada, *©Gary Hamburgh / Gary Hamburgh Photography*

DUCK

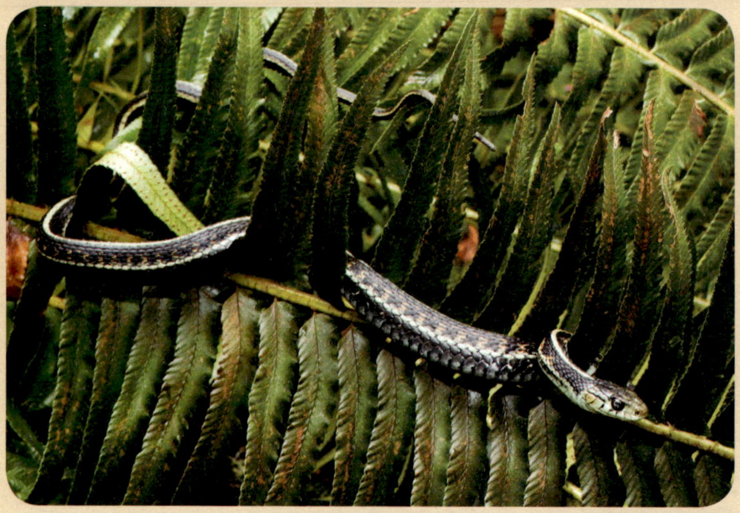

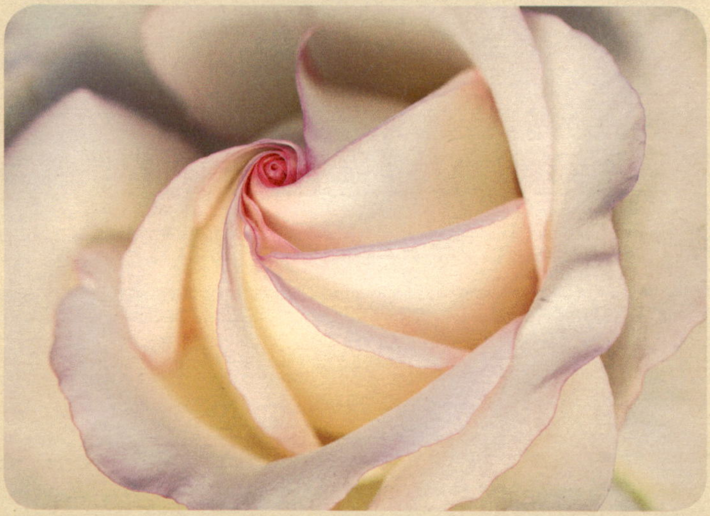

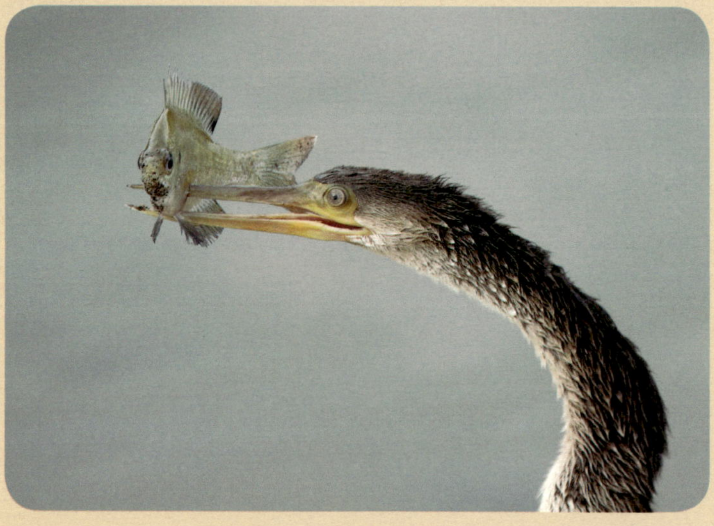

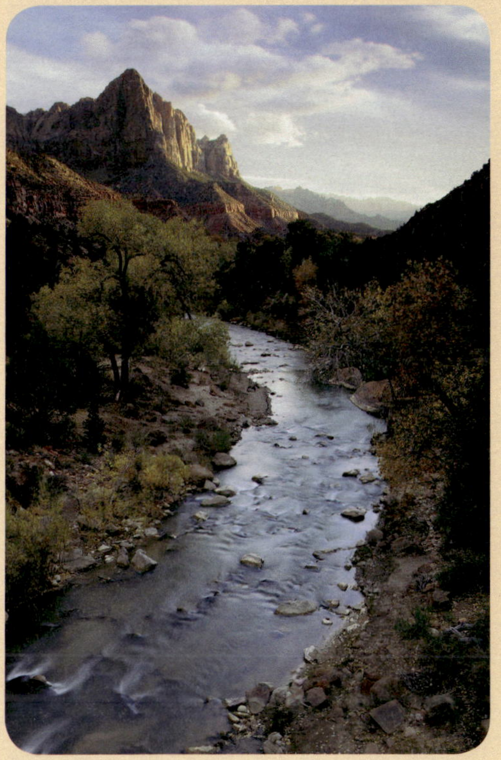

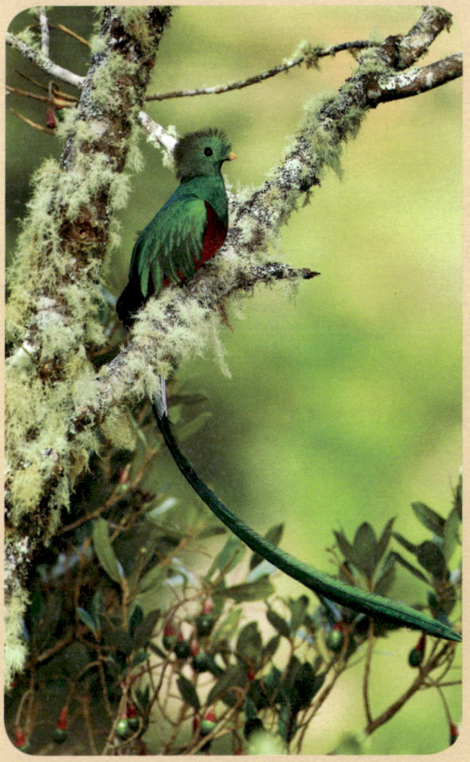

LEFT

Top:
Garter Snake and Ferns, Cape Disappointment State Park, Washington, *©Bill Gozansky / Bill Gozansky Photography*

Middle:
Moonstone Hybrid Tea Rose Petals in Spiral, Lincolnwood, Illinois, *©Erwin Barrington*

Bottom:
Anhinga with Fresh Catch, Everglades National Park, Florida, *©Alfred Forns*

RIGHT

Top:
Virgin River Liquid Ribbon, Zion National Park, Utah, *©Ronald Heusser*

Bottom:
Resplendant Quetzal in Costa Rica, *©Annie Katz / Annie Katz Photography*

TWIST

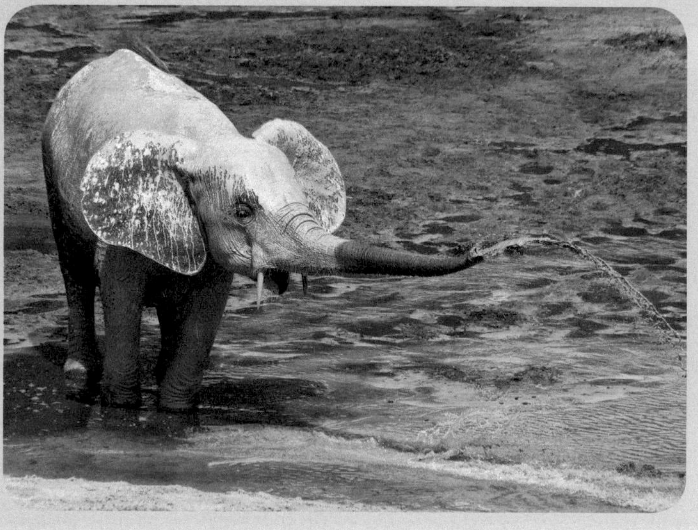

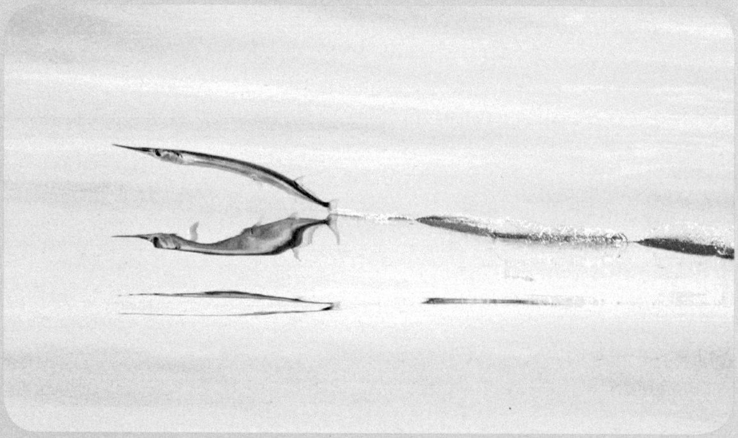

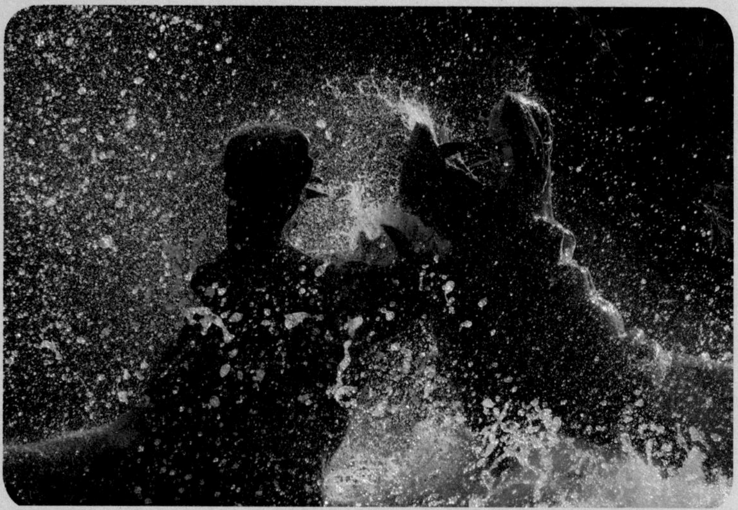

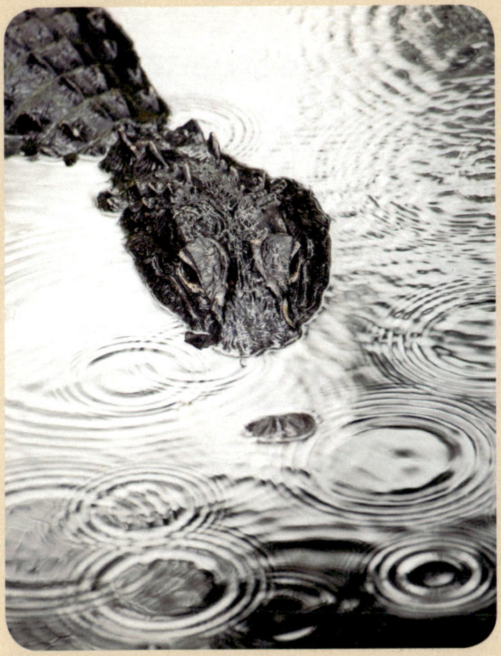

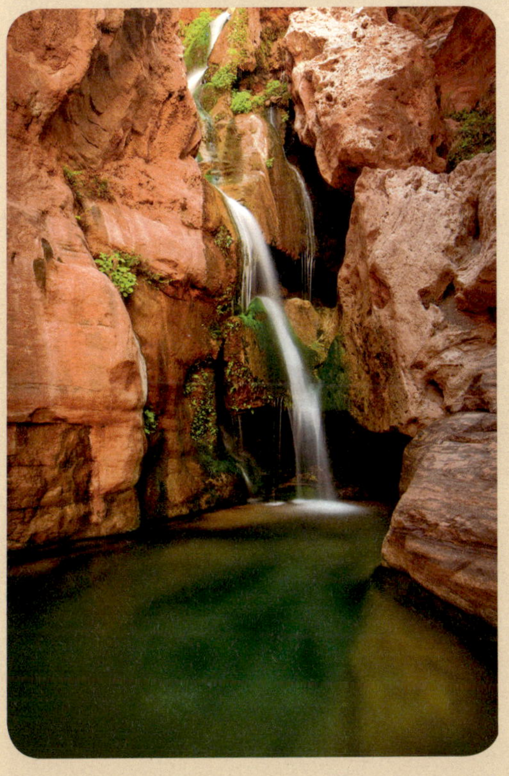

LEFT

Top:
African Forest Elephant Digging for Mineral Salts, Dzanga Sangha Reserve, Central African Republic, *©Cynthia Walpole / focus frog, LLC*

Middle:
Atlantic Houndfish Skipping Water Surface, Dry Tortugas, Florida, *©Shawn Marques / Shoot To Thrill Images*

Bottom:
Hippo Battle on the Sabie River, Kruger National Park, South Africa, *©Steve Mandel*

RIGHT

Top:
Alligator in the Rain, Everglades National Park, Florida, *©Thomas Wood*

Bottom:
Elves Chasm Waterfall, Grand Canyon National Park, Arizona, *©Josh Miller / Josh Miller Photography*

SPLASH

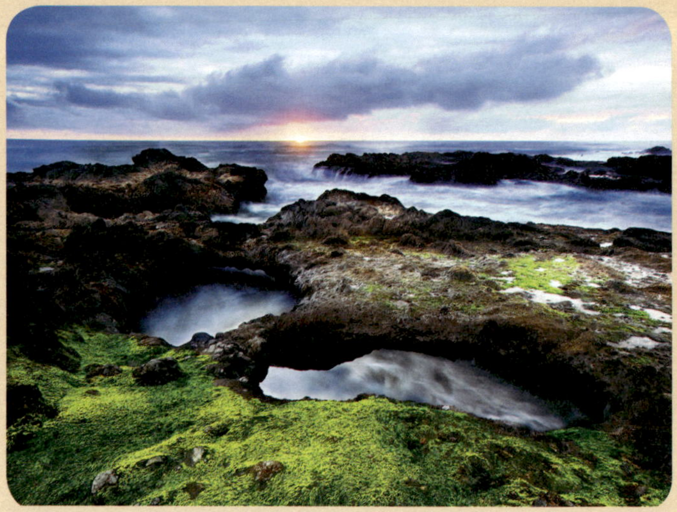

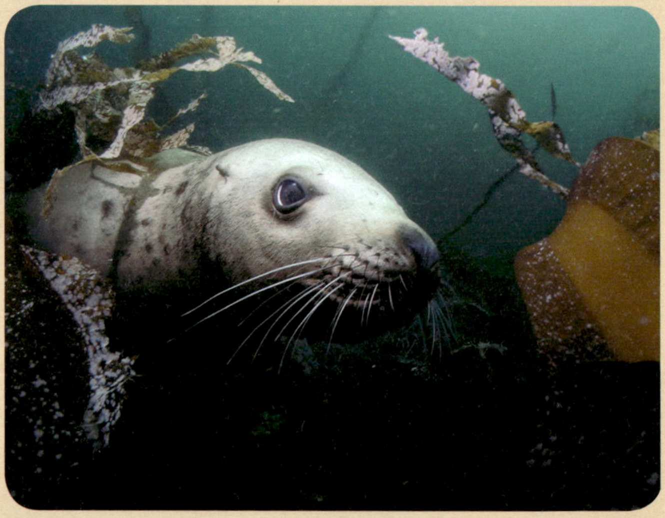

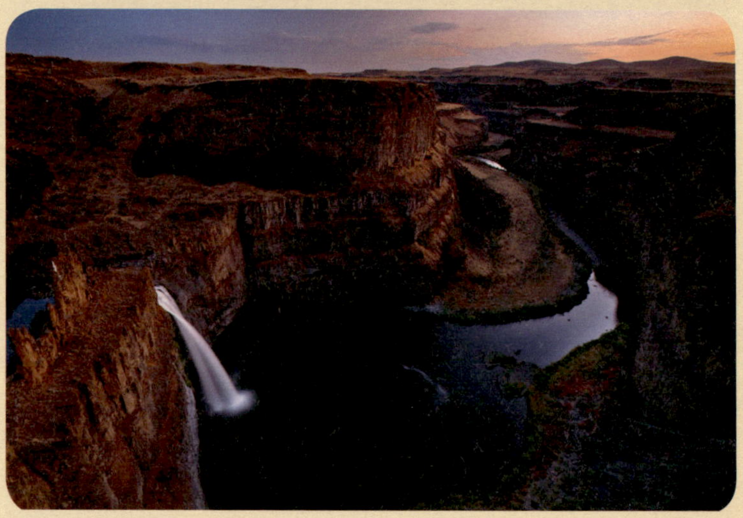

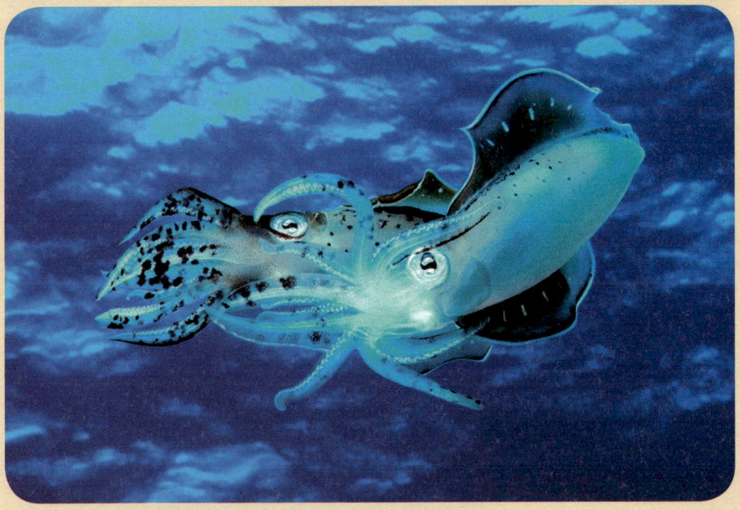

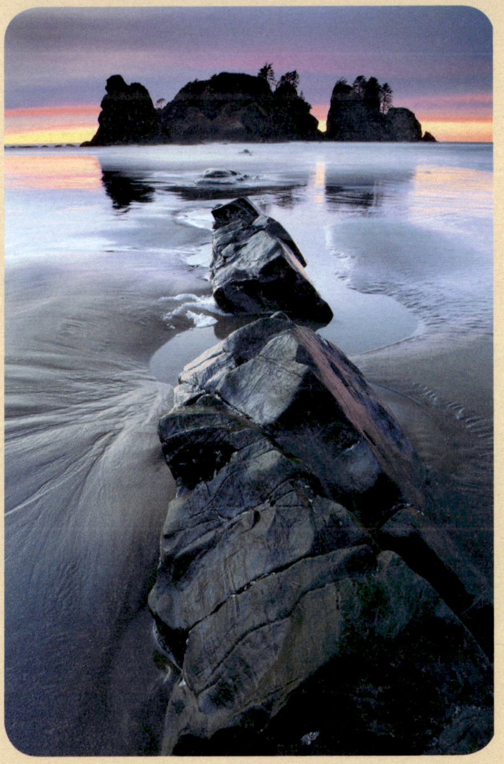

LEFT

Top:
Yachats Beach, Yachats State Park, Oregon, ©*Ashley Adams*

Middle:
Stellar Sea Lion, Yasha Island, Alaska, ©*Bryce Flynn*

Bottom:
Twilight Falls, Palouse Falls, Washington, ©*Sean Bagshaw / Outdoor Exposure Photography, LLC*

RIGHT

Top:
Mating Caribbean Reef Squids, Curacao, Netherlands Antilles, ©*Barry Brown / Missing Pieces*

Bottom:
Leading to Light, Point of the Arches, Olympic National Park, Washington, ©*Geoffrey Schmid / Geoffrey Schmid Photographic Images*

AQUATIC

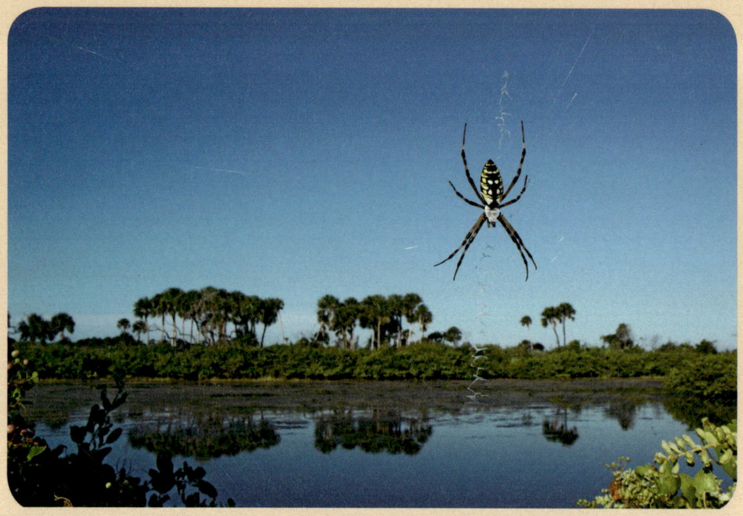

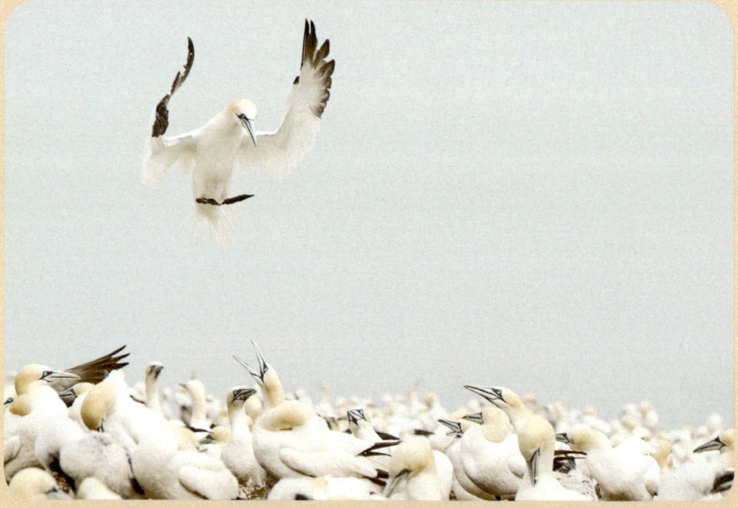

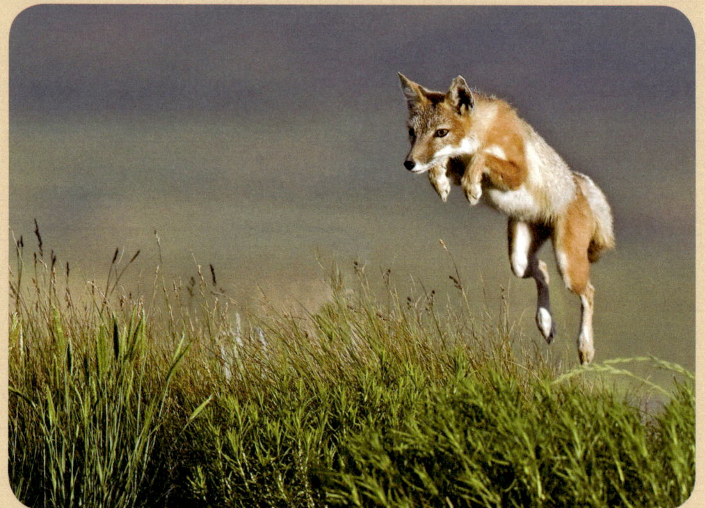

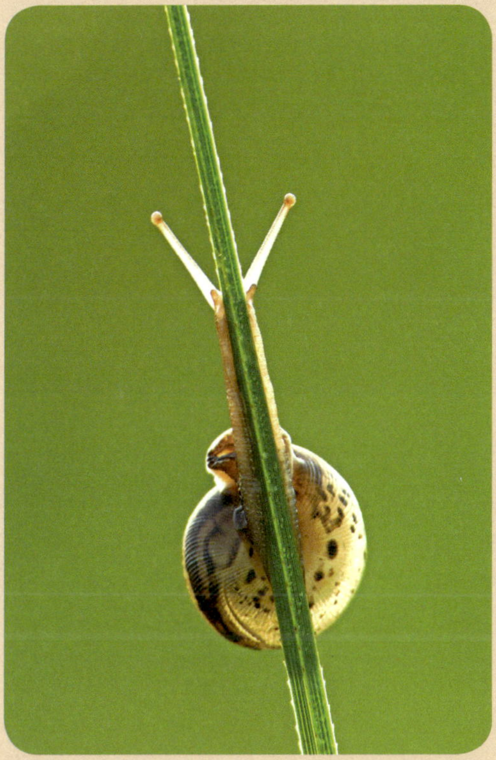

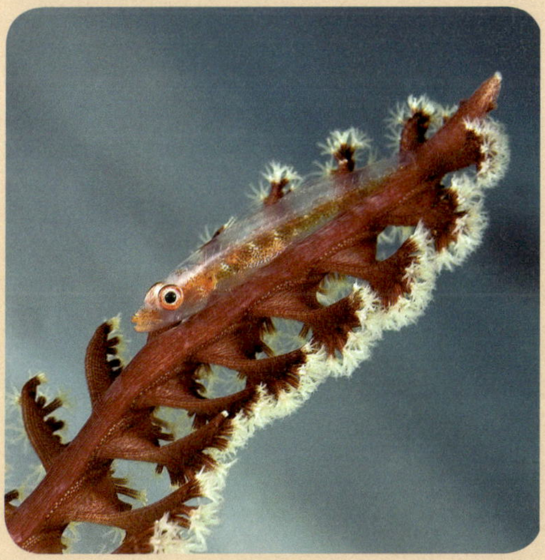

LEFT

Top:
Banana Spider Overlooking Lagoon, Merritt Island National Wildlife Refuge, Florida, *©Robert Amoruso / Wildscape Images*

Middle:
Northern Gannet, Bonaventure Island, Quebec, Canada, *©Michael Milicia / Michael Milicia Photography*

Bottom:
Swift Fox, Shirley Basin near Casper, Wyoming, *©Jim Brown*

RIGHT

Top:
Morning Crawl, Big Cypress National Preserve, Florida, *©Kevin Barry*

Bottom:
Goby on Seapen, Wakatobi, Indonesia, *©Ricky Ferguson / Fotos N Fins*

ABOVE

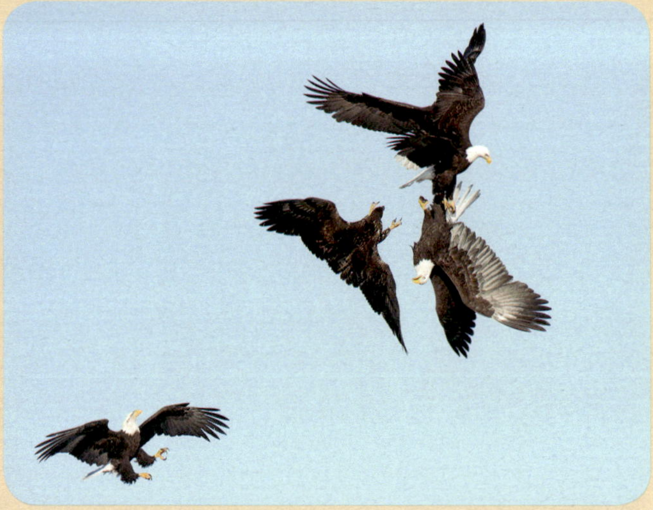

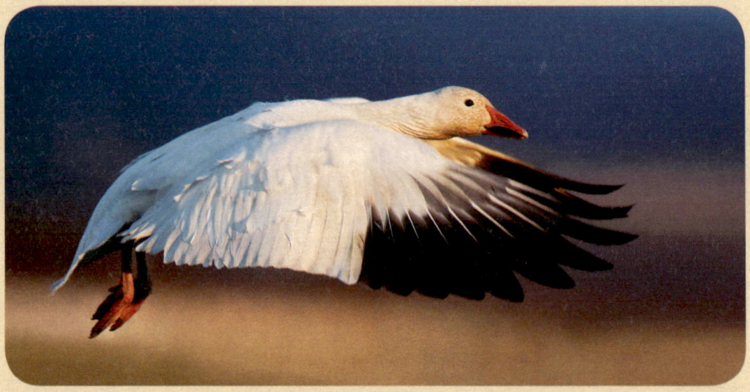

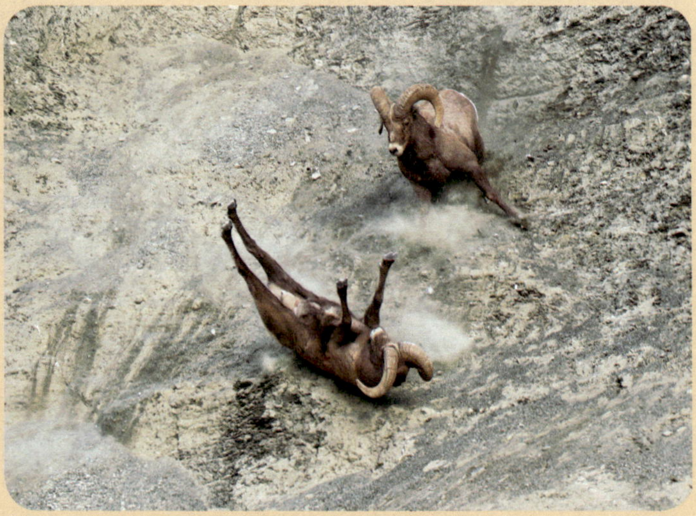

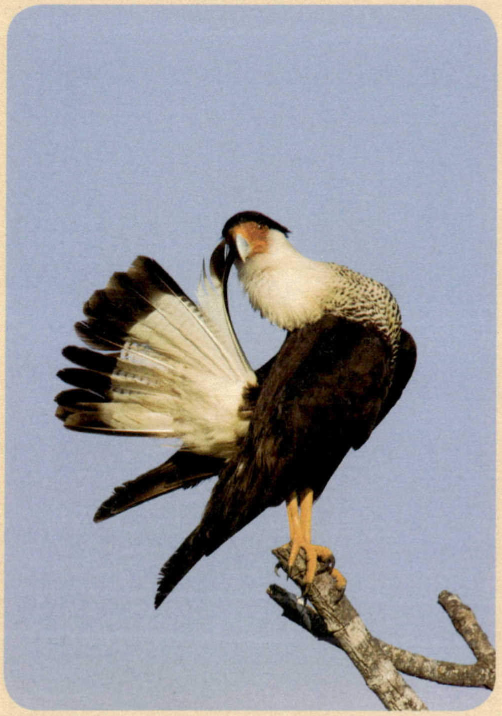

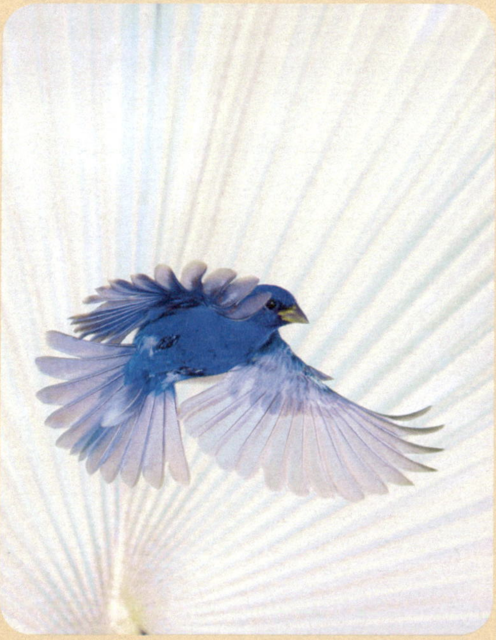

LEFT

Top:
Bald Eagle Combat, Homer, Alaska, *©Bill Harbin*

Middle:
Sunset Flight of the Snow Goose, Fir Island, Washington, *©Bonnie Block / Field and Farm Photography*

Bottom:
Bighorn Sheep Knocked Over During Rut, Yellowstone National Park, Montana, *©Thomas Stanton*

RIGHT

Top:
Crested Caracara Preening, Hidalgo County, Texas, *©Greg Lasley*

Bottom:
Indigo Bunting in Flight, Immokalee, Florida, *©Bernard Friel / a different perspective*

FLIGHT

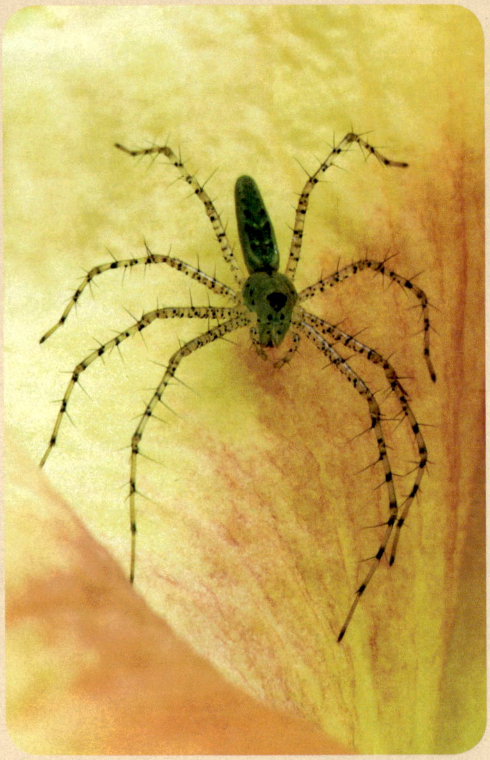

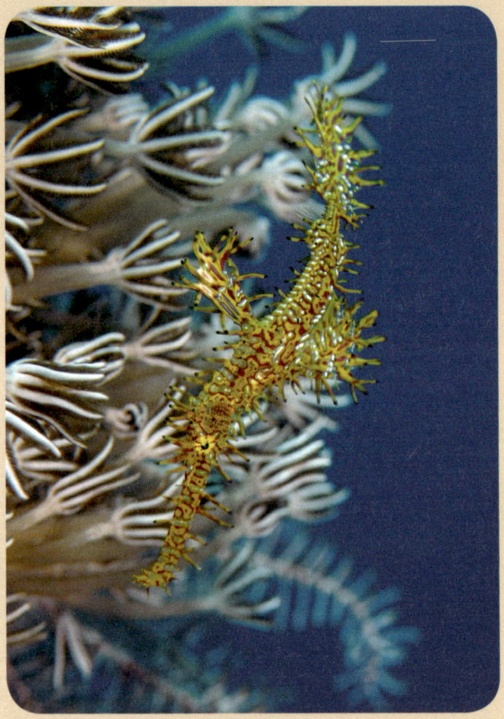

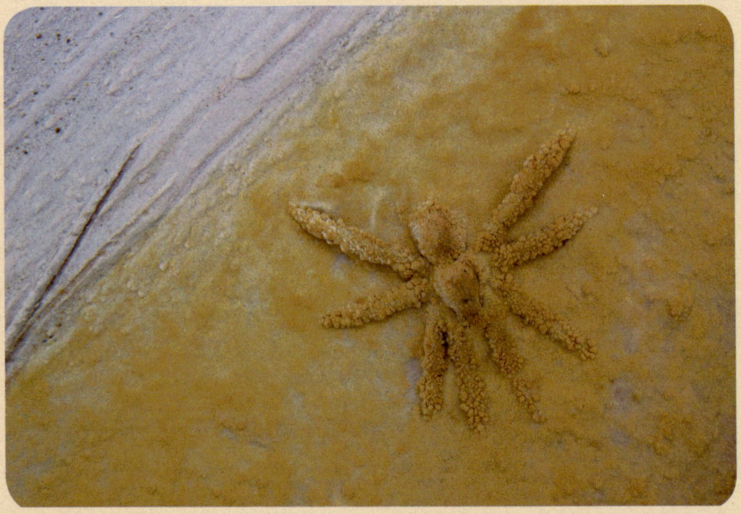

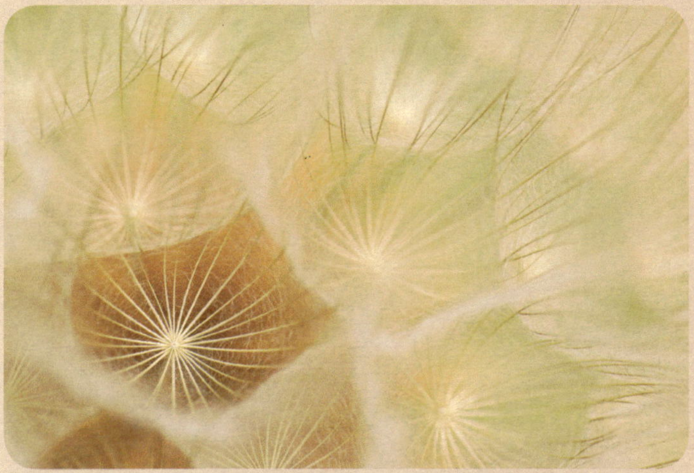

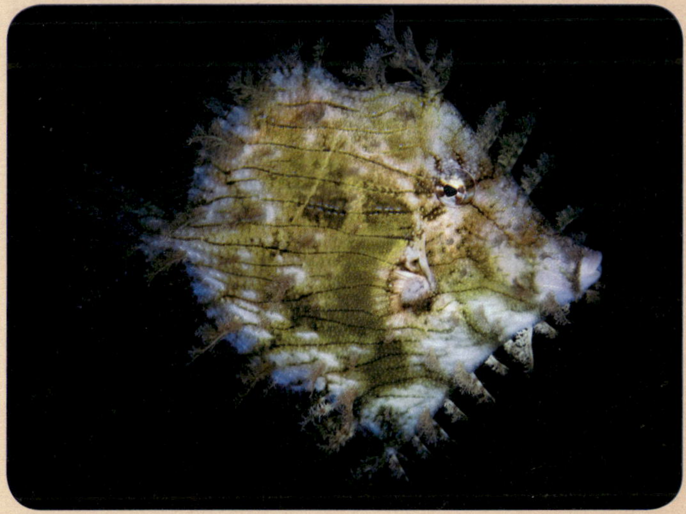

LEFT

Clockwise from top left:

Spider on Flower, Savannah, Georgia, *©Joanne Wells*

Ornate Ghostpipefish, Dumaguete, Philippines, *©Ricky Ferguson / Fotos N Fins*

Thermophilic Spider in Thermal Pool, Yellowstone National Park, Wyoming, *©Jeff Vanuga / Vanuga Photography*

RIGHT

Top:

Dandelion Puff at Roadside, near Denver, Colorado, *©Jamie Konarski Davidson / New Life Photos*

Bottom:

Leafy Filefish, Lembeh Strait, North Sulawesi, Indonesia, *©Christopher Crowley*

EXTENSIONS

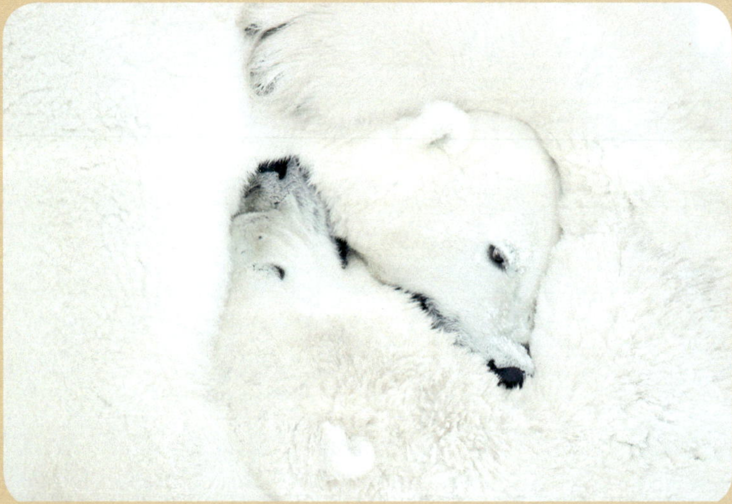

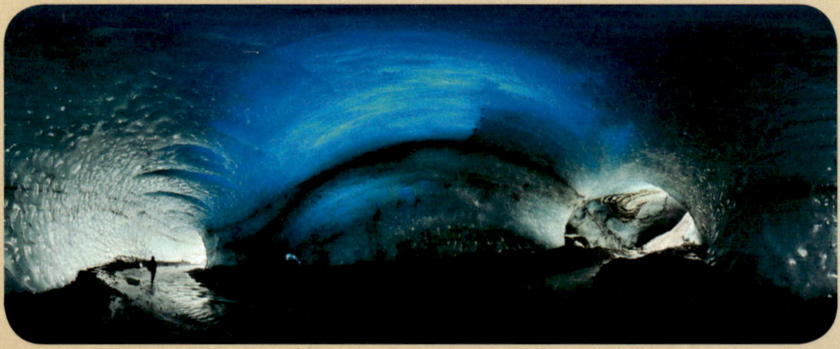

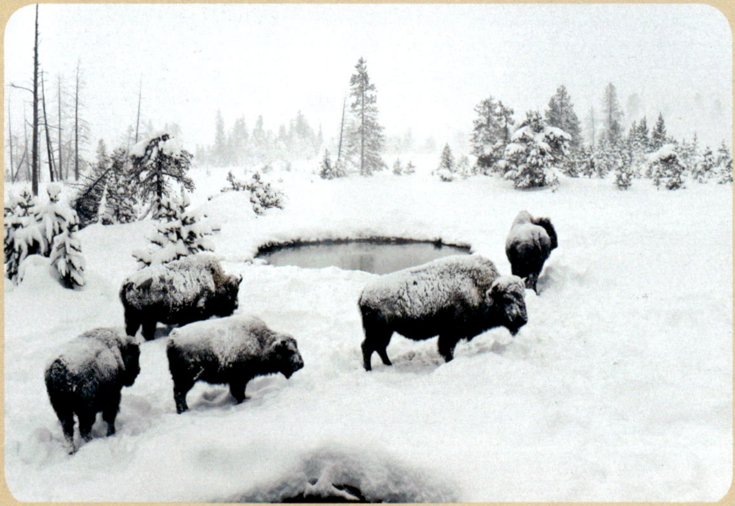

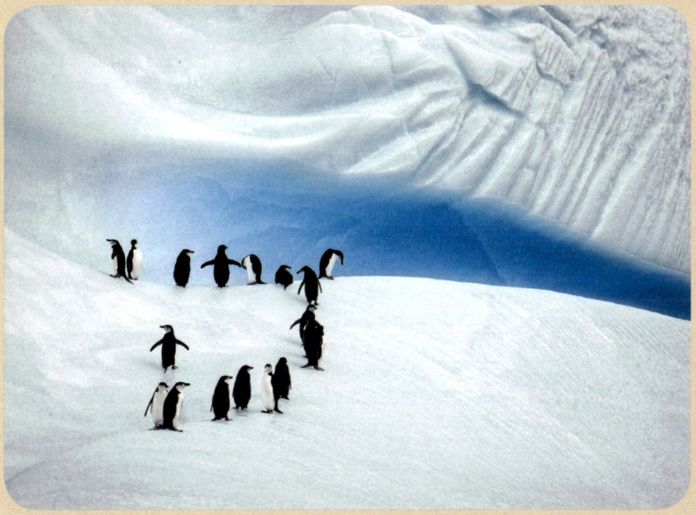

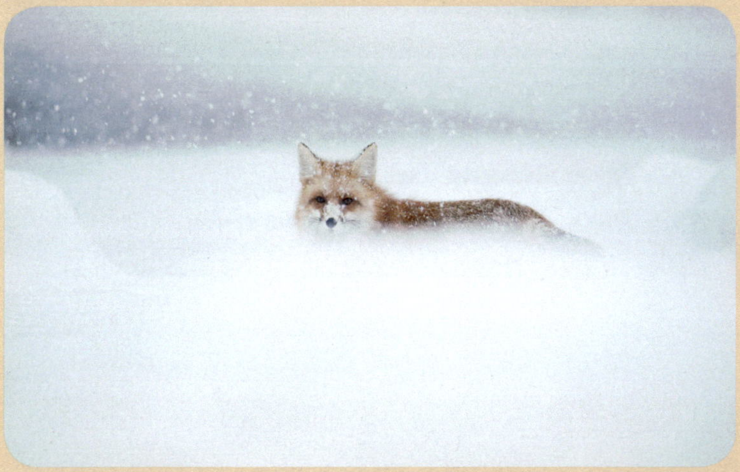

LEFT

Top:
Polar Bear Hug, Wapusk National Park, Canada, *©Daisy Gilardini*

Middle:
Explorer in Kverkfjöll Ice Caves, Northern Vatnajökull Glacier, Iceland (Phil), *©Johnathan Esper / Wildernesscapes Photography*

Bottom:
Buffalo, Yellowstone National Park, Montana, *©Nancy Damron*

RIGHT

Top:
Chinstrap Penguins on Iceberg, South Atlantic Ocean, *©Greg Ferguson / Greg Ferguson Photography*

Bottom:
Mountain Fox, Yellowstone, Wyoming, *©Fabiola Forns*

COLD

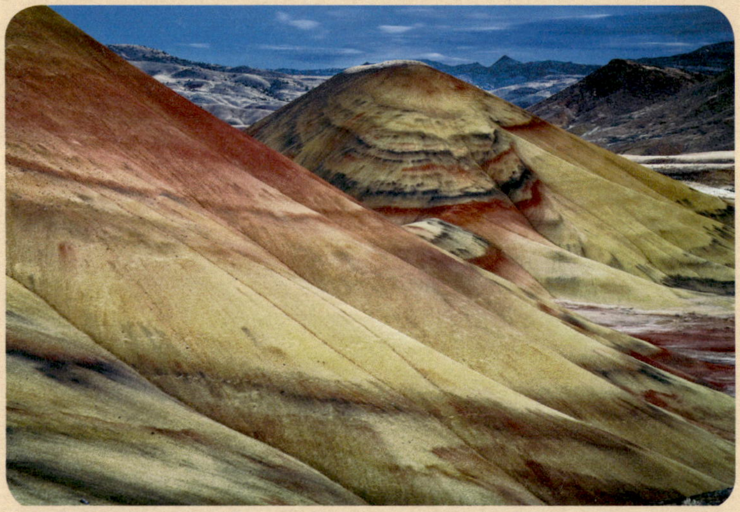

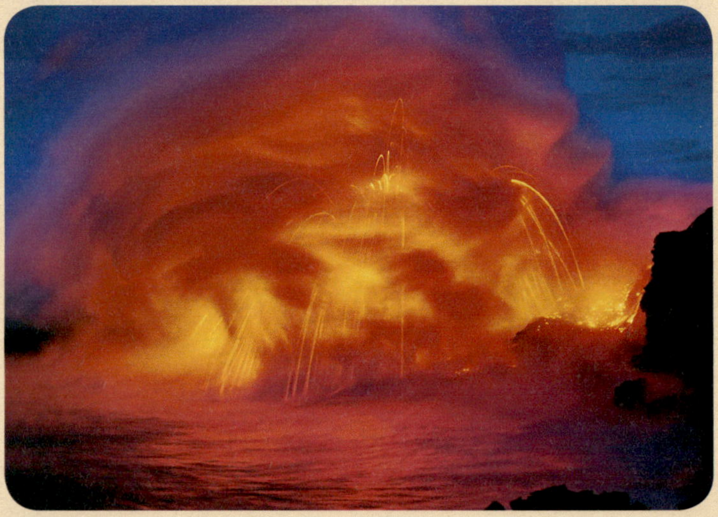

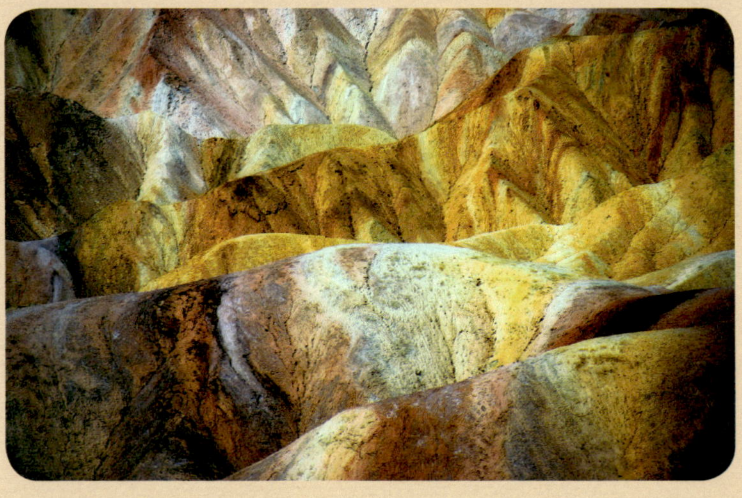

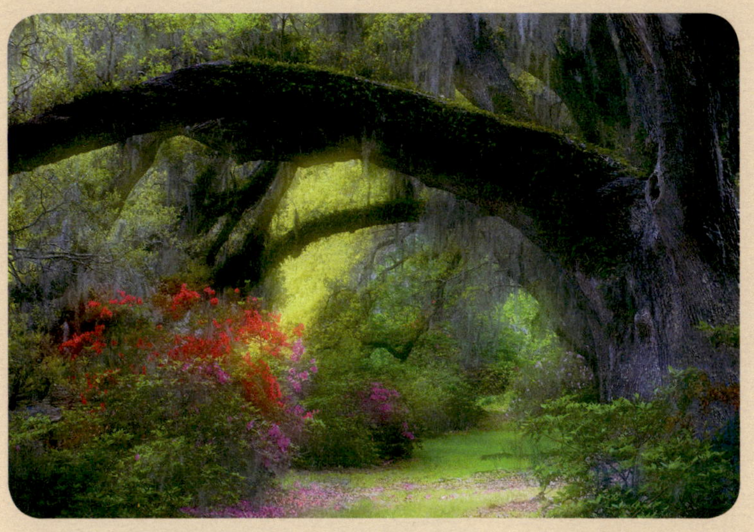

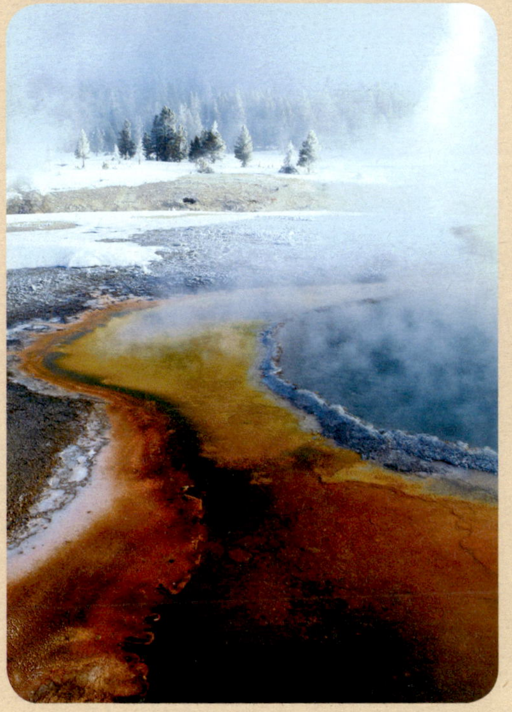

LEFT

Top:
Painted Hills, John Day Fossil Beds National Monument, Oregon (Phil), *©Sean Bagshaw / Outdoor Exposure Photography, LLC*

Middle:
Kilauea Volcano, the Big Island, Hawaii, *©Peter Lik*

Bottom:
Desert Sandstorm at Zabriskie Point, Death Valley National Park, California, *©Trixi Huish / Trixi Huish Photography*

RIGHT

Top:
Magnolia Gardens Double Exposure, Magnolia Gardens, South Carolina (Phil), *©Nancy Rotenberg / Natural Tapestries*

Bottom:
Winter Hot Pools, Yellowstone National Park, Wyoming, *©Dan Leffel*

PAINT

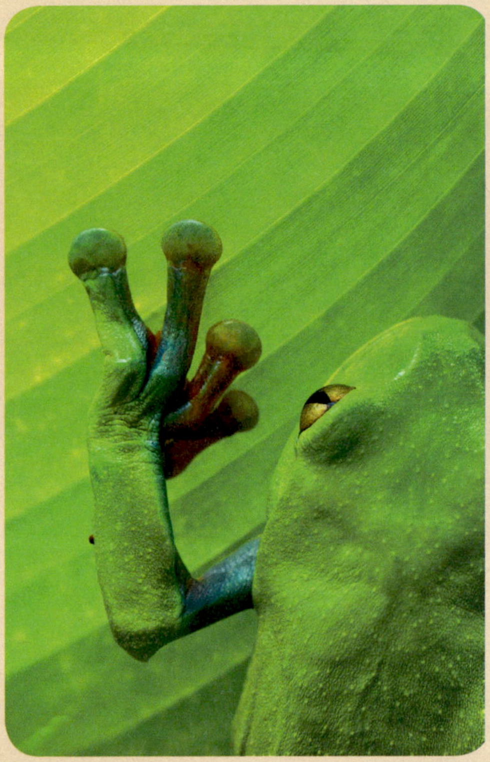

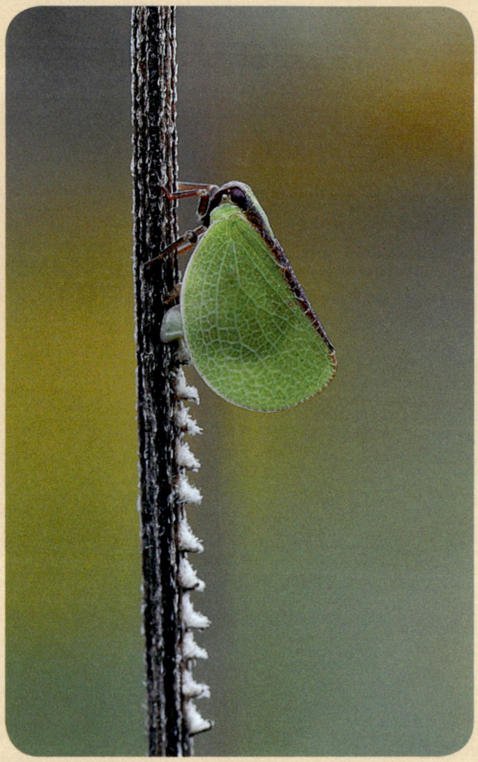

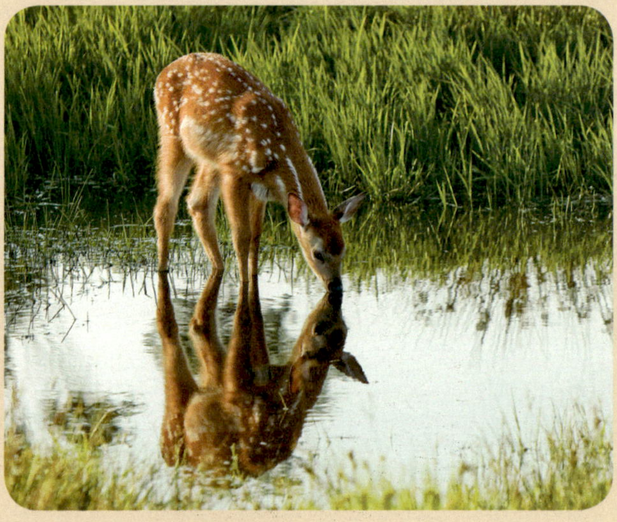

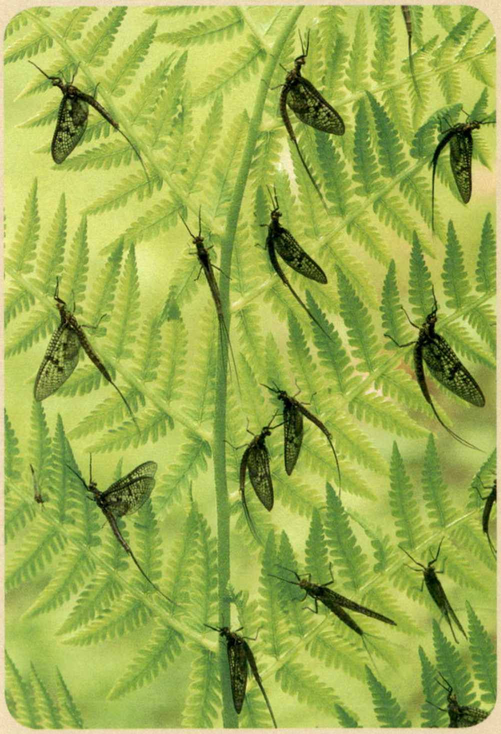

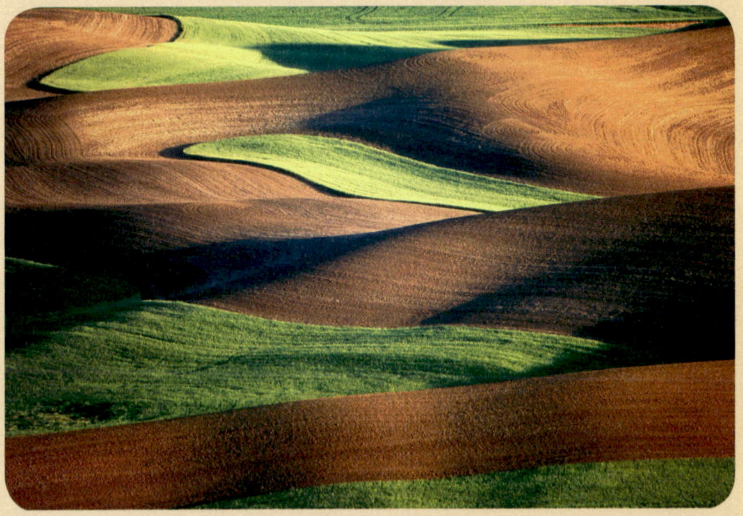

LEFT

Clockwise from top left:

Tree Frog with Toes, Costa Rica, *©Nancy Rotenberg / Natural Tapestries*

Leaf Hopper Laying Eggs, Jackson County, Michigan, *©Robert Domm / Robert Domm Photography*

Morning Reflections, Shenandoah National Park, Virginia, *©Wil Hershberger / Nature Images and Sounds*

RIGHT

Top:

Mayflies on Fern, Jackson County, Michigan, *©Robert Domm / Robert Domm Photography*

Bottom:

Plowed Hills, The Palouse, Washington, *©Eleanor Briccetti*

GREEN

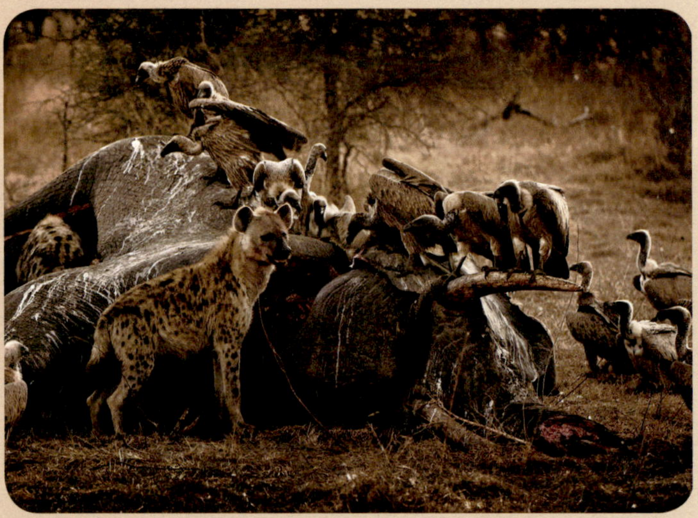

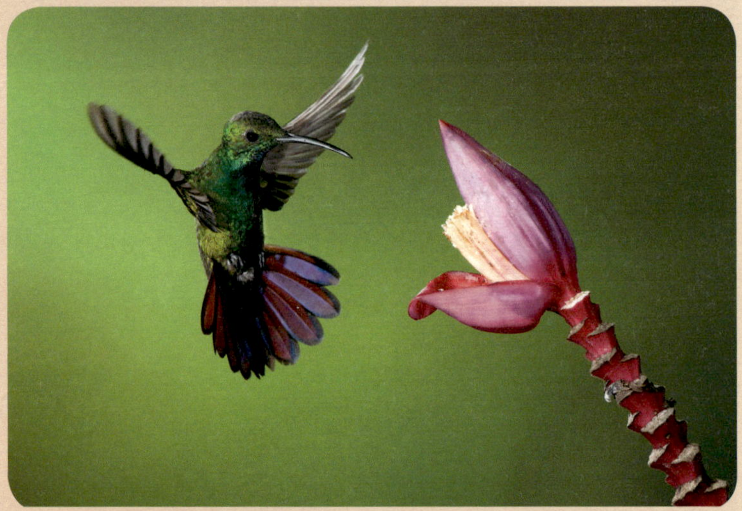

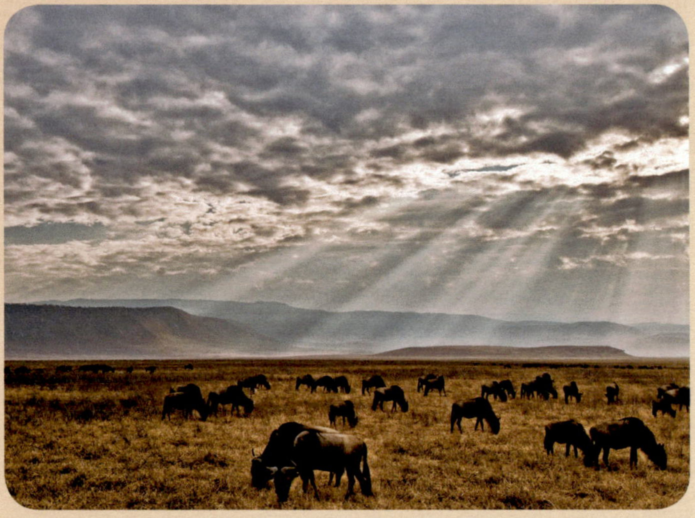

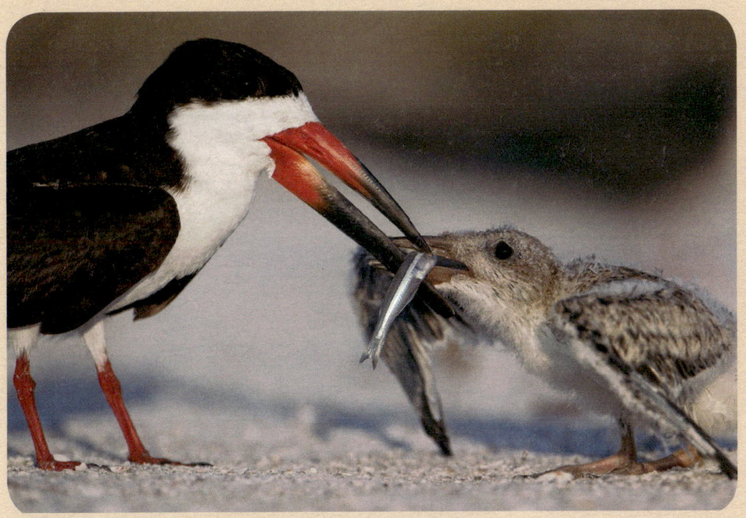

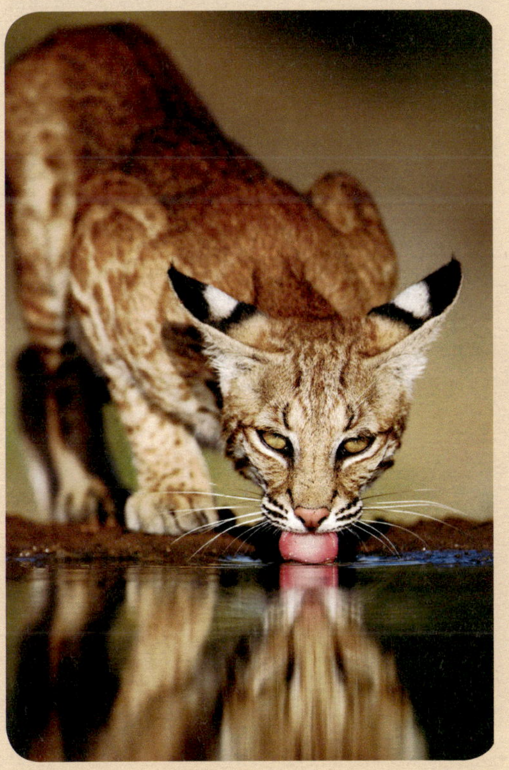

LEFT

Top:
Death in the Bushveld, Mala Mala, South Africa, *©Chris Gray / Shades of Gray*

Middle:
Green-Breasted Mango Hummingbird, Rancho Naturalista, Costa Rica, *©Keith Bauer*

Bottom:
Wildebeests at Morning, Ngorongoro Crater, Tanzania, *©Donna Eaton / Donna Eaton Photography*

RIGHT

Top:
Black Skimmer Fish Transfer, Indian Shores, Florida, *©Christina Evans / ChromaGraphics Studios, Inc.*

Bottom:
Bobcat at Waterhole, Santa Clara Ranch, South Texas, *©Jeremy Woodhouse / PixelChrome, Inc.*

FEED

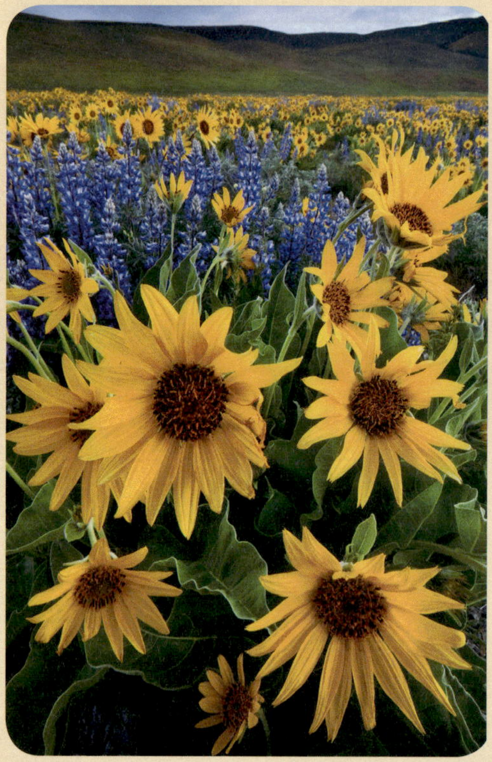

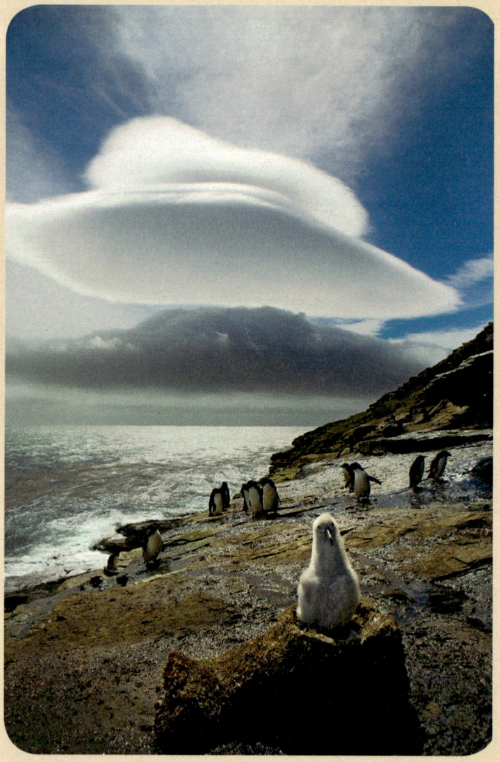

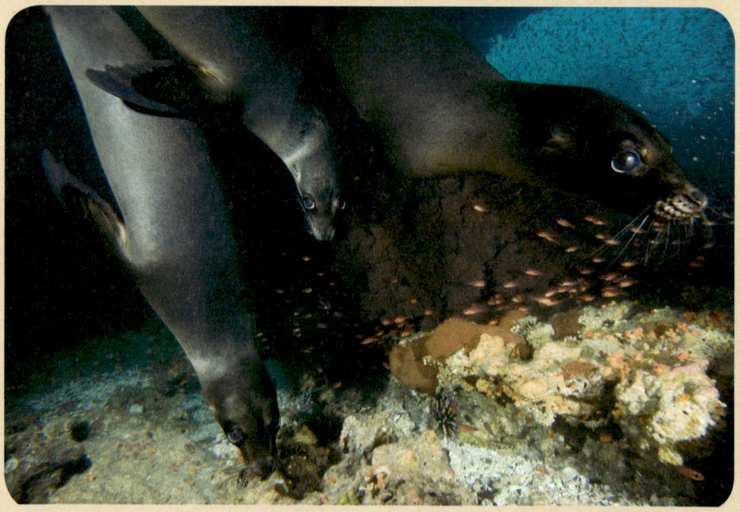

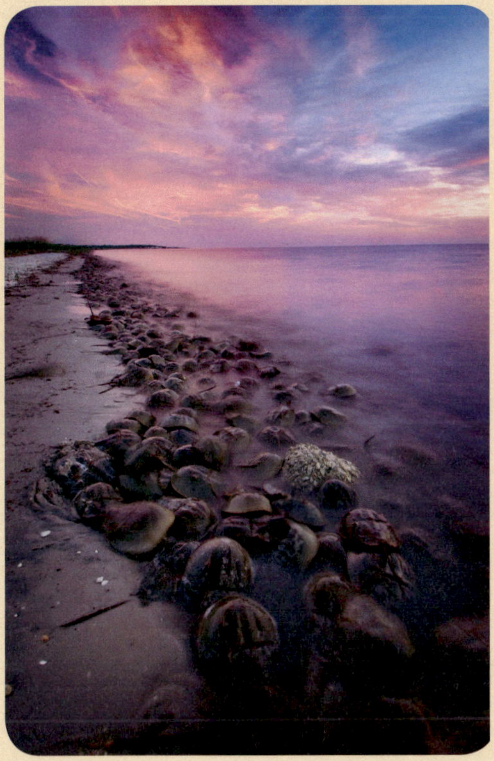

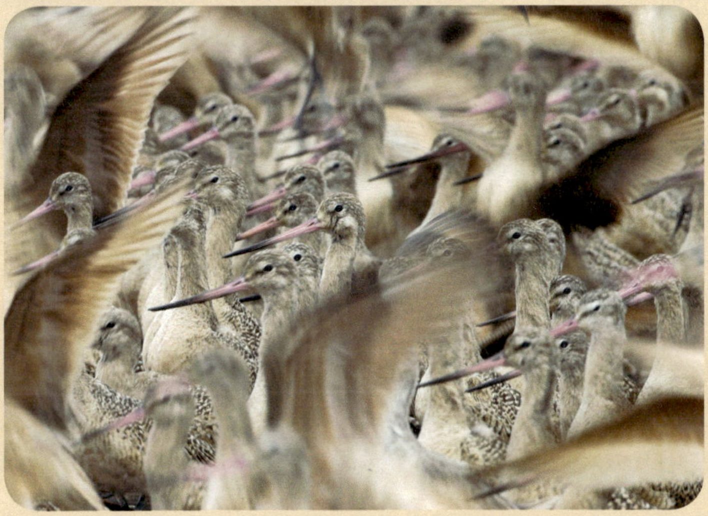

LEFT

Clockwise from top left:

Balsam Root and Lupine, Dalles Mountain Ranch, Washington, *©Sean Bagshaw / Outdoor Exposure Photography, LLC*

Lenticular Cloud, Falkland Islands, South Atlantic Ocean, *©Mark Lissick / Wildlight Nature Photography*

Galapagos Sea Lions in Underwater Cave, Santa Fe Island, Galapagos Islands, Ecuador, *©Matthew Meier / Matthew Meier Photography*

RIGHT

Top:

Horseshoe Crabs Storm the Beach, Delaware Bay, New Jersey, *©Joseph Rossbach / Joseph Rossbach Photography*

Bottom:

Marbled Godwits, Willapa Bay, Washington, *©Nathan Chappell / Trogon Tours, Inc.*

CROWD

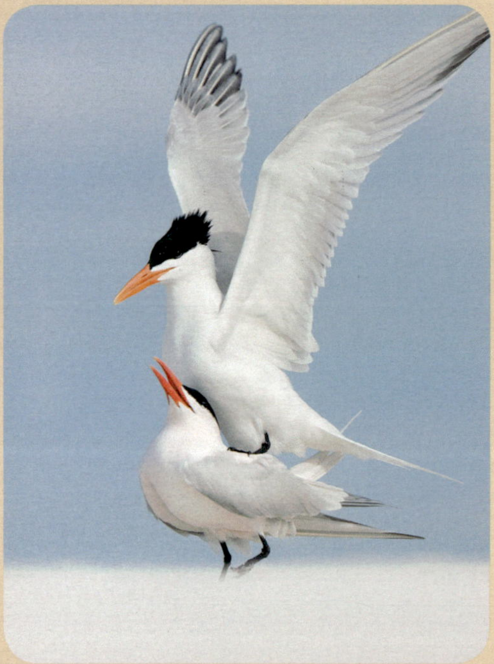

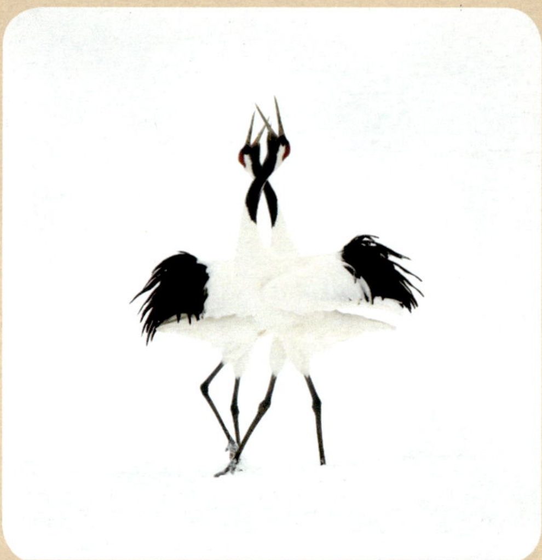

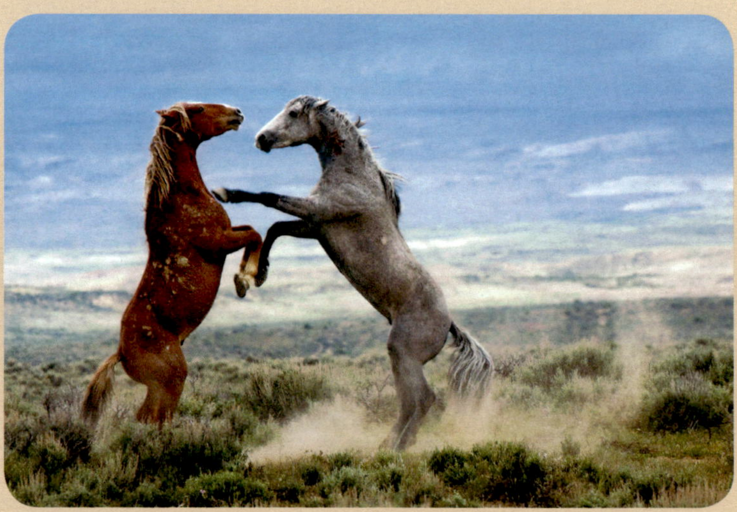

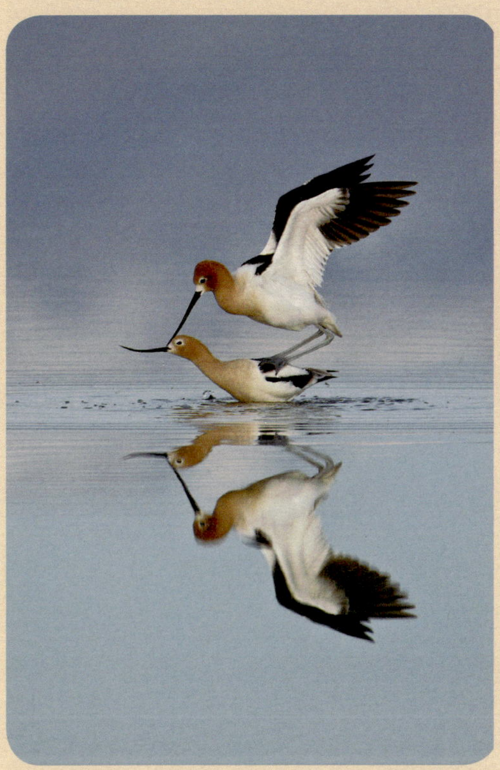

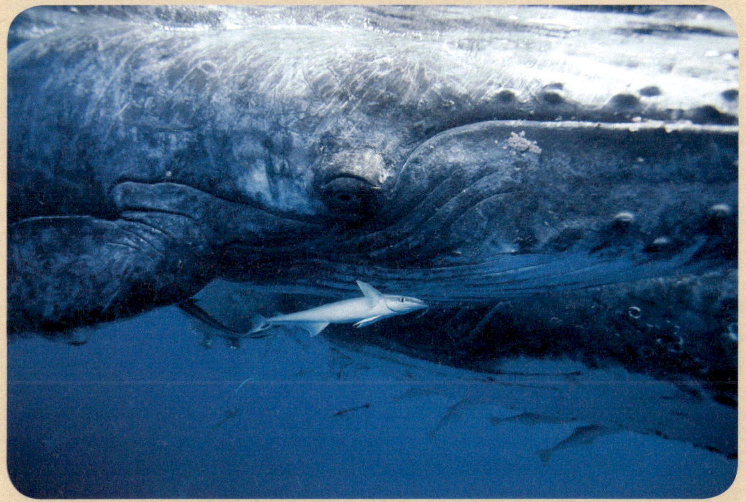

JUDGE'S CHOICE

LEFT

Clockwise from top left:
Royal Terns Mating, Fort De Soto Park, St. Petersburg, Florida, *©David Kennedy*

The Dance Performed by Cranes, Hokkaido, Japan, *©Mark Lagrange*

Fighting Wild Stallions, Bureau of Land Management Land, Wyoming, *©Carol Glazer / Glazer Creative Group*

RIGHT

Top:
American Avocets Mating, Antelope Island State Park, Utah, *©James Hager / James Hager Photography*

Bottom:
Humpback Calf with Mother and Remora, Vava'u Islands, Tonga, *©Sue Flood / Tartan Dragon Ltd.*

PARTNER

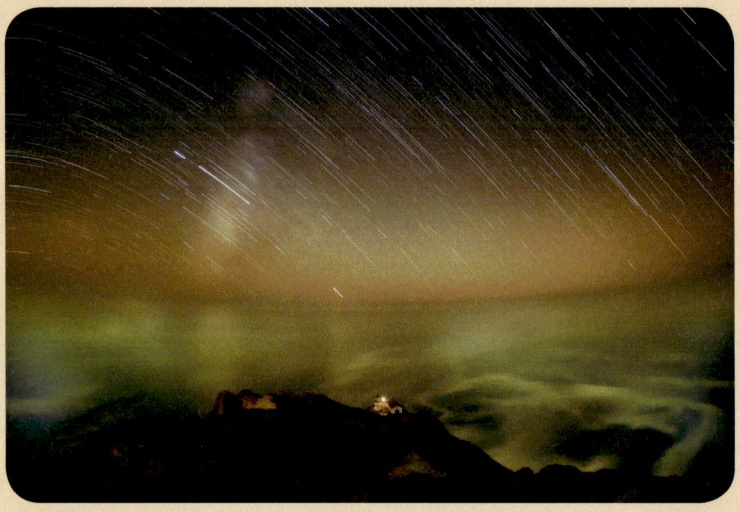

JUDGE'S CHOICE

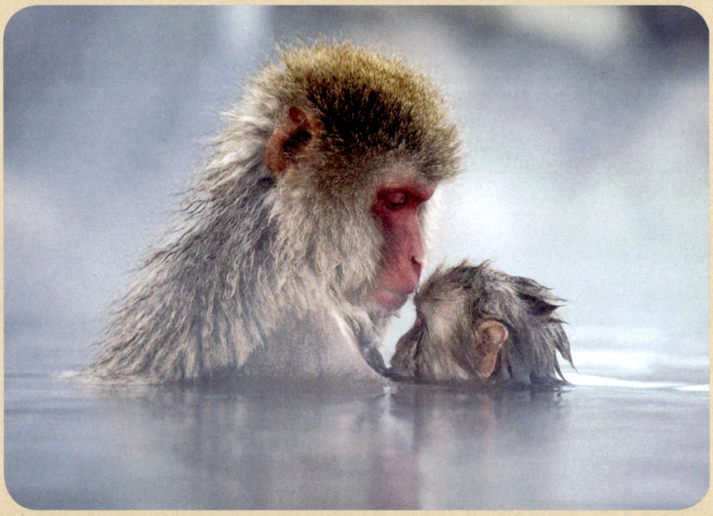

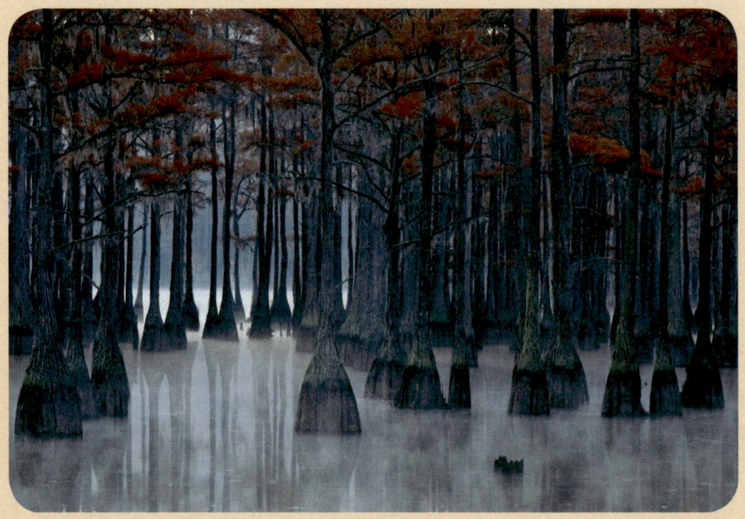

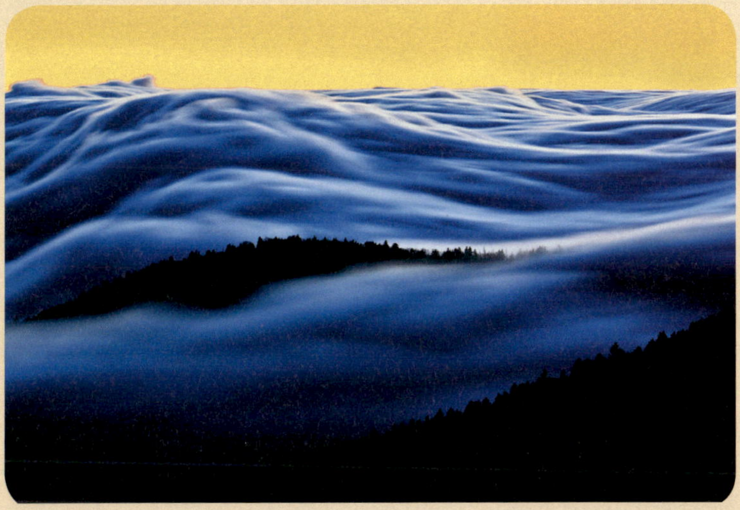

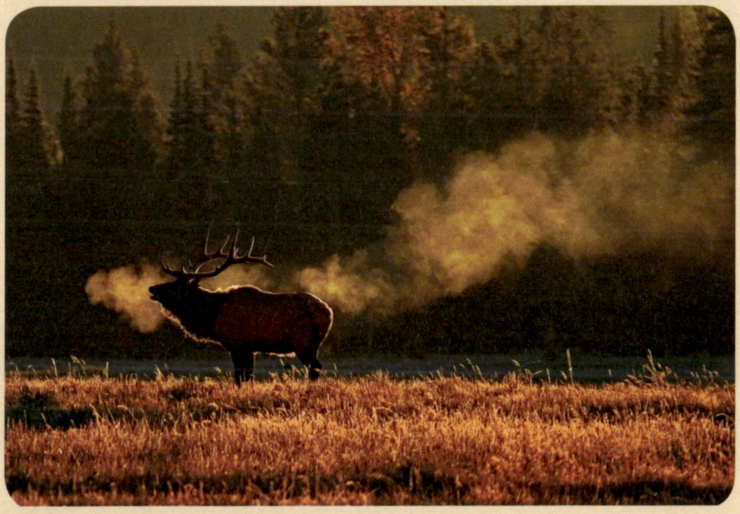

LEFT

Top:
Edge of Night, Point Reyes National Seashore, California (Phil), *©Harold Davis*

Middle:
Japanese Macaques, Nagano, Japan, *©Steve Mandel*

Bottom:
Cypress Trees in Fall, George Smith State Park, Georgia, *©Maria Struss*

RIGHT

Top:
Mountain Tops and Rushing Clouds at Dusk, Clingmans Dome, Great Smoky Mountains, Tennessee, *©Joseph Rossbach / Joseph Rossbach Photography*

Bottom:
Elk Bugling on Cold Morning, Grand Teton National Park, Wyoming, *©Thomas Stanton*

FOG

JUDGE'S CHOICE

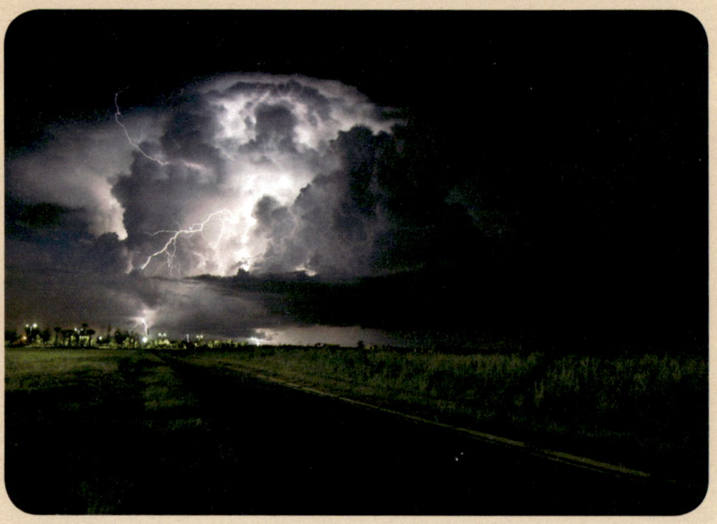

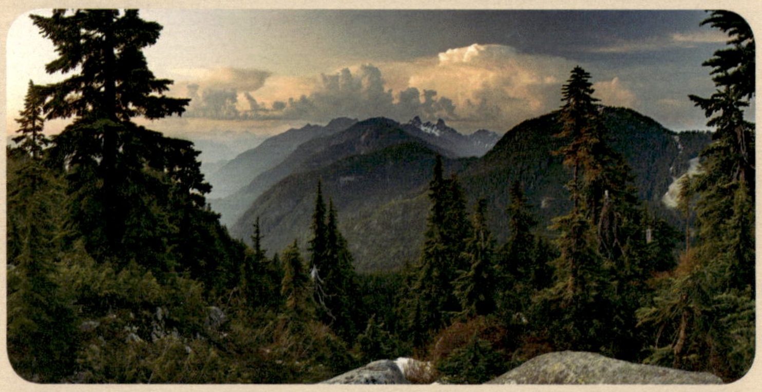

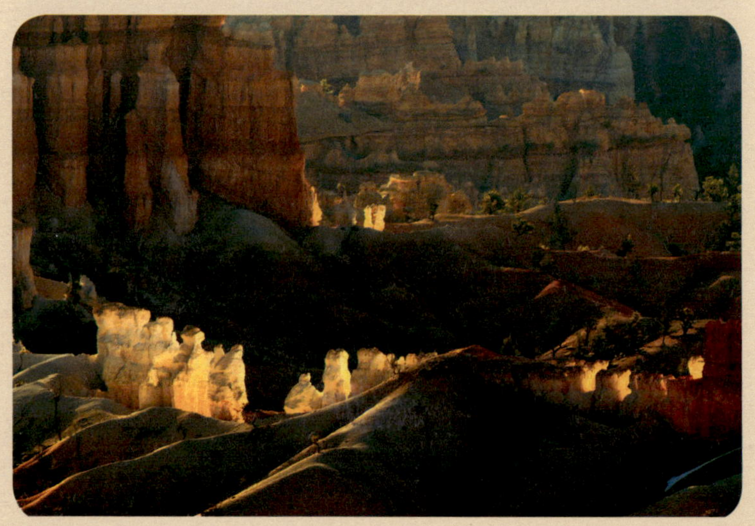

JUDGE'S CHOICE

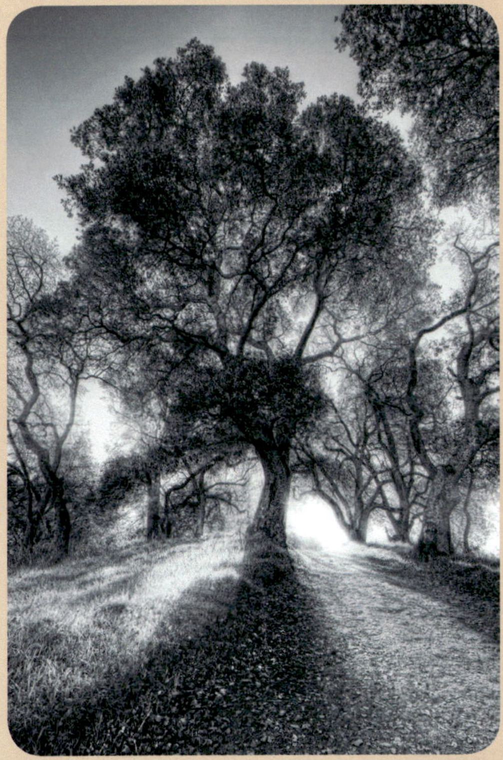

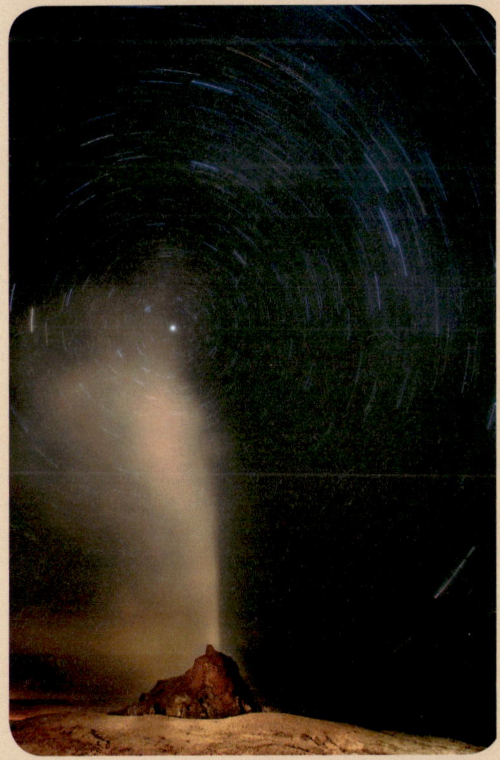

LEFT

Top:
Lightning Storm In Starry Sky, Port St. Lucie, Florida, *©Shawn Marques / Shoot To Thrill Images*

Middle:
Howe Sound Crest from Black Mountain at Sunset, Cypress Regional Park, British Columbia (Phil), *©David Johnston*

Bottom:
Back Glow on Bryce Hoodoos, Bryce Canyon National Park, Utah, *©Chuck Haney / Chuck Haney Outdoor Photography*

RIGHT

Top:
Winter Light, Lafayette, California, *©Kelly Cannon*

Bottom:
White Dome Geyser Night Eruption, Yellowstone National Park, Wyoming, *©Roman Kurywczak / Roamin with Roman Photo Tours*

LIGHT

Clockwise from top left:

Red-eyed Treefrog, Costa Rica, *©Dan Suzio / Dan Suzio Photography*

Screaming Snail Kite in Flight, Loxahatchee, Florida, *©Alfred Forns*

Bobcat Displaying Flemming Response, Sunol Regional Wilderness, California, *©Robert Stronck / pixel-gym*

Indigo Bunting at Birdbath, Rochester, Minnesota, *©Michael Henry*

Barn Swallow Nestlings Calling to Mom for Food, Littleton, Colorado, *©Clinton Shoemaker, Jr.*

SING

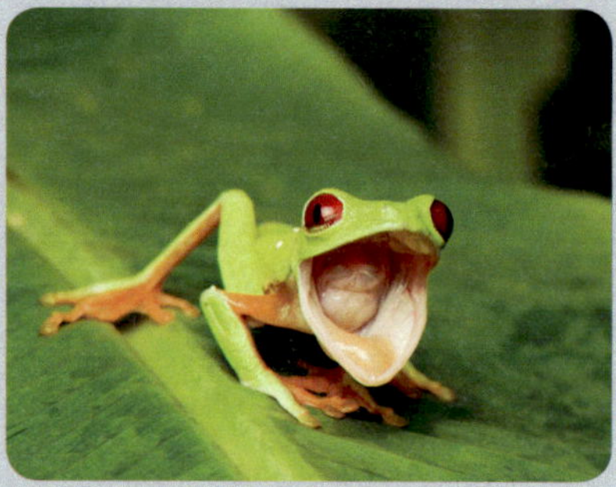

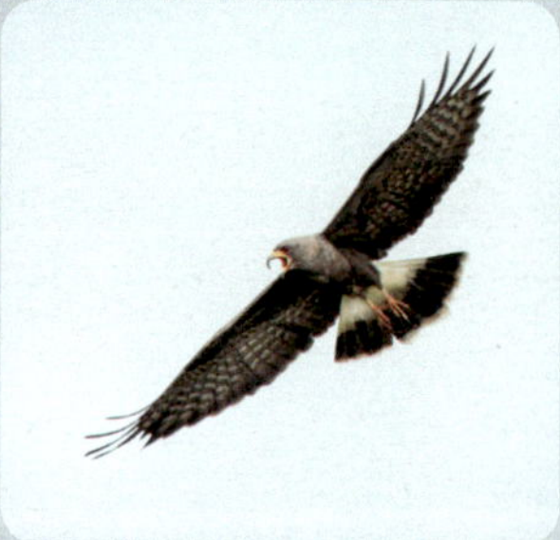

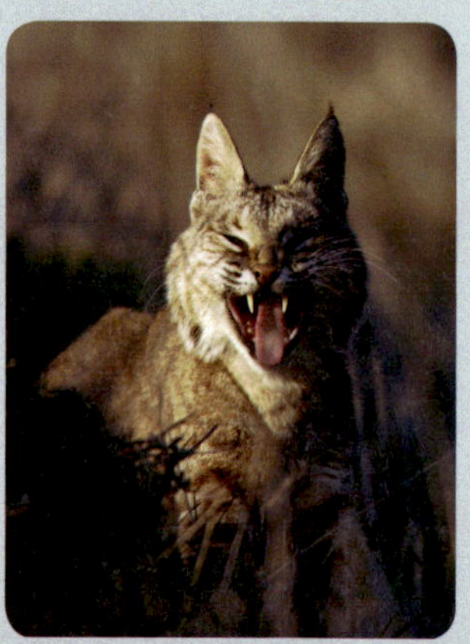

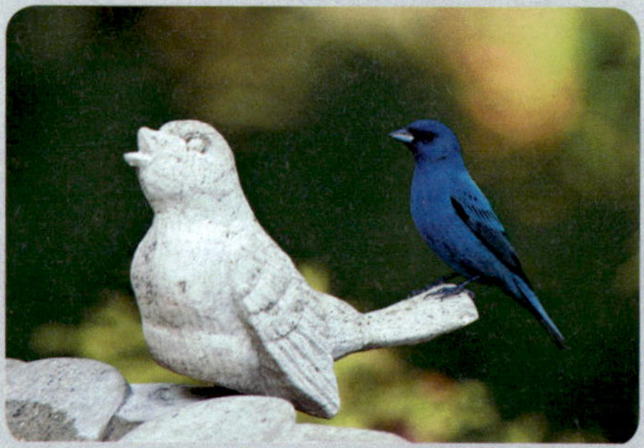

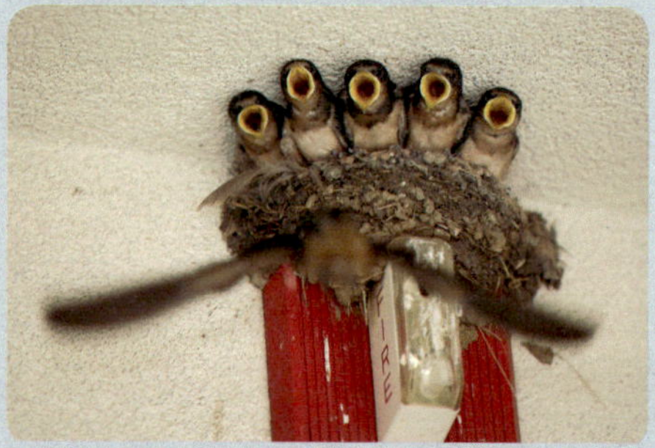

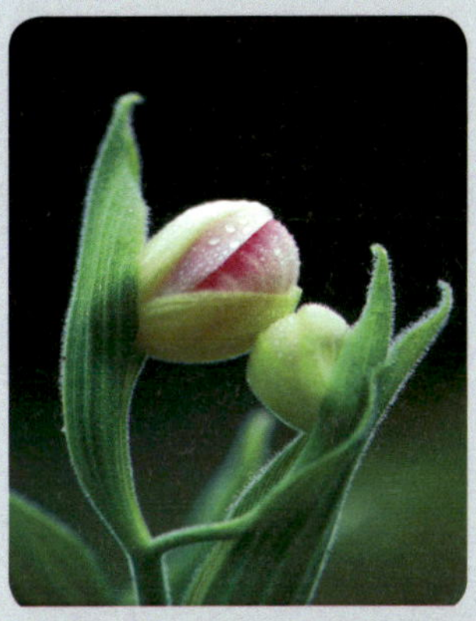

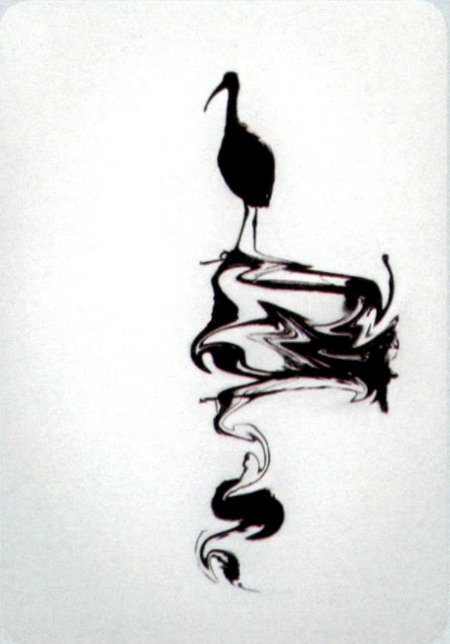

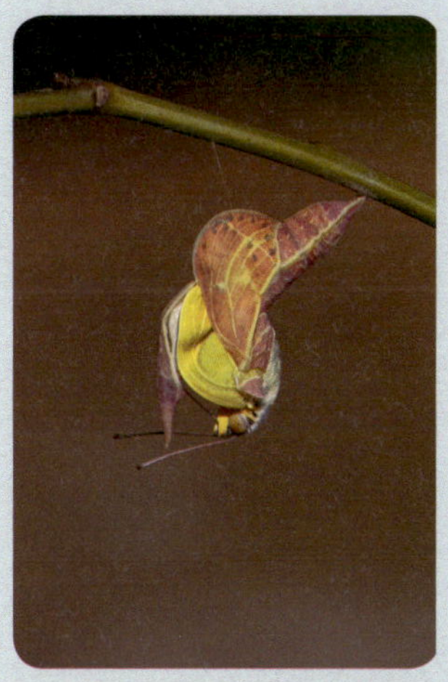

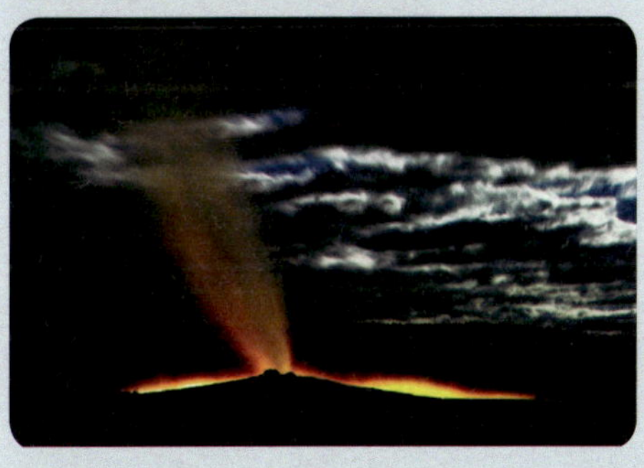

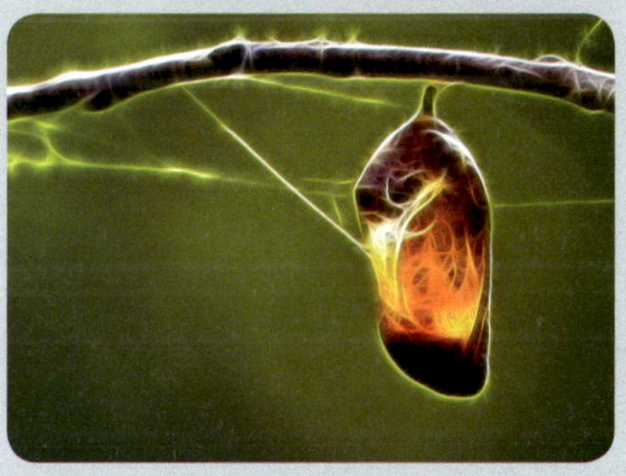

Clockwise from top left:

Pink Lady Slipper Buds in Rain, Bruce Peninsula, Ontario, Canada, *©Nancy Rotenberg / Natural Tapestries*

Ibis and Swirled Reflection, Farmington Bay Wildlife Refuge, Utah (Phil), *©Gerald Johnson*

Orange-Barred Sulphur Butterfly Emergence, Largo, Florida, *©Christina Evans / ChromaGraphics Studios, Inc.*

Transformations, Coral Springs, Florida (Phil), *©Daniel Grove*

Old Faithful after Eruption, with Rim Light, Yellowstone National Park, Wyoming, *©Thomas Stanton*

TRANSFORM

Clockwise from top left:

Anemone Stomach, Palau, *©Larissa Roorda*

Bush Katydid, Pink Color Morph, Killdeer Plains Wildlife Area, Wyandot County, Ohio (Capt), *©David FitzSimmons / FitzSimmons Photography*

Roseate Spoonbill Take-off, Tampa Bay, Florida, *©Fabiola Forns*

Argiope Spider with Prey, Sarah P. Duke Gardens, Durham, North Carolina, *©Jamie Konarski Davidson / New Life Photos*

Dawn Breaks over Mather Gorge, Great Falls National Park, Virginia, *©Joseph Rossbach / Joseph Rossbach Photography*

PINK

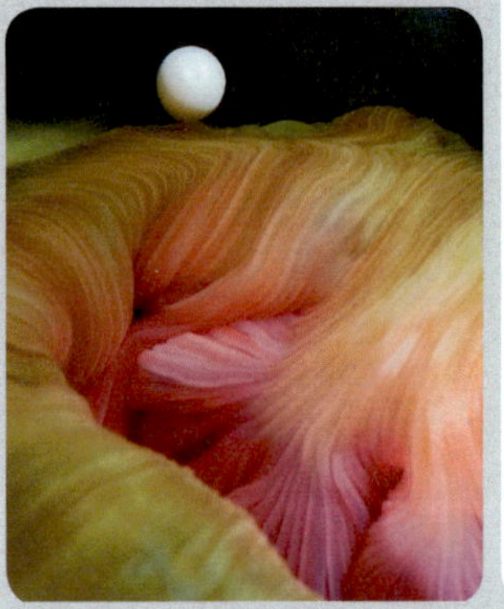

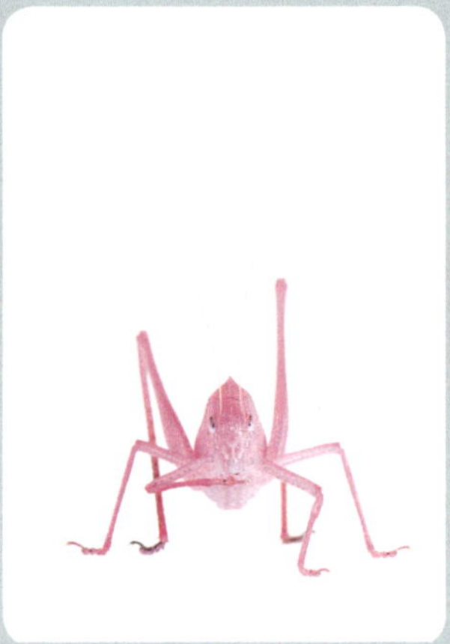

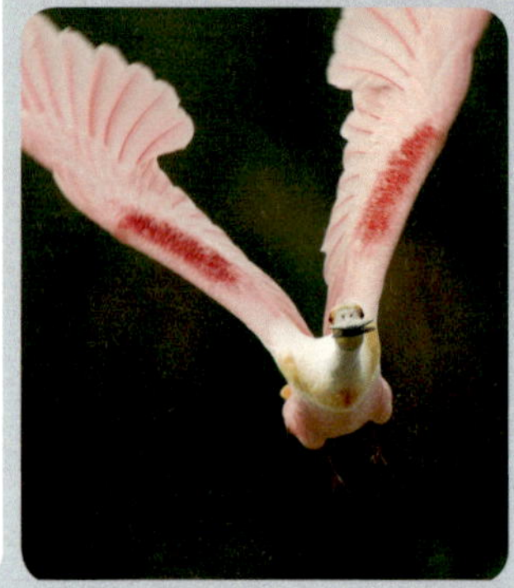

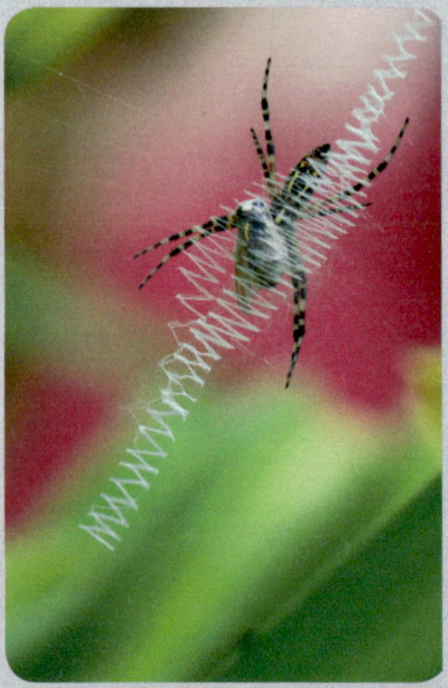

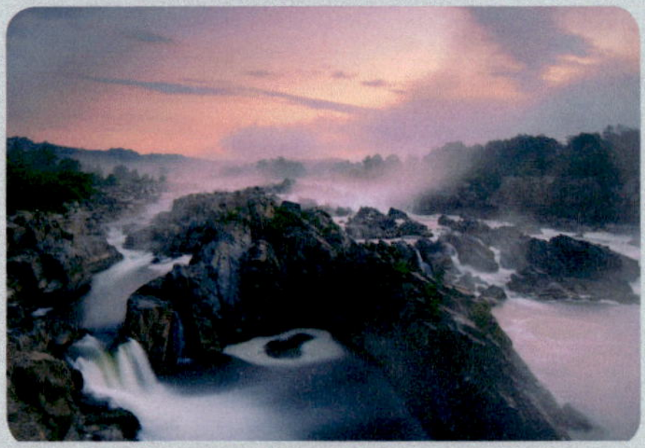

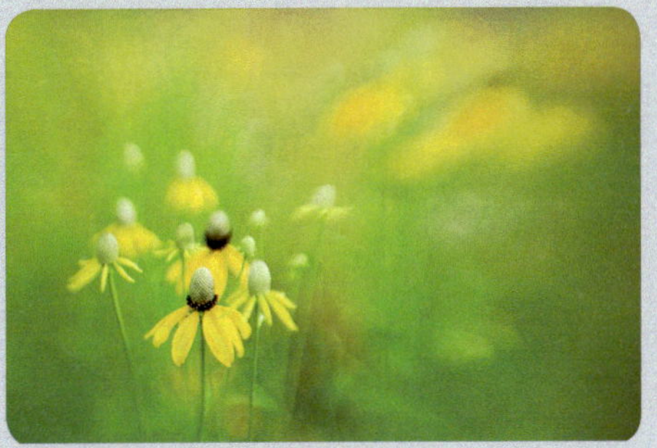

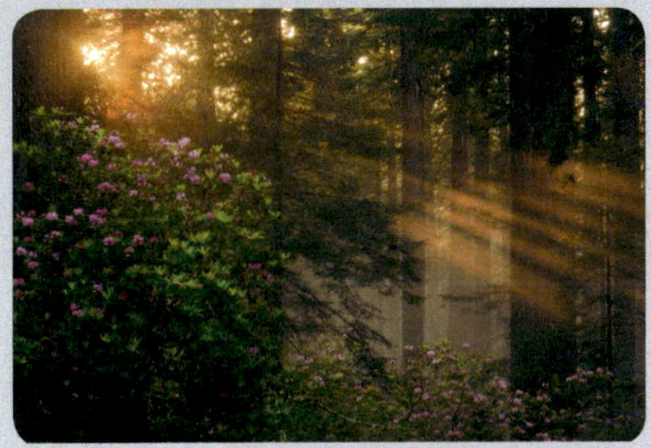

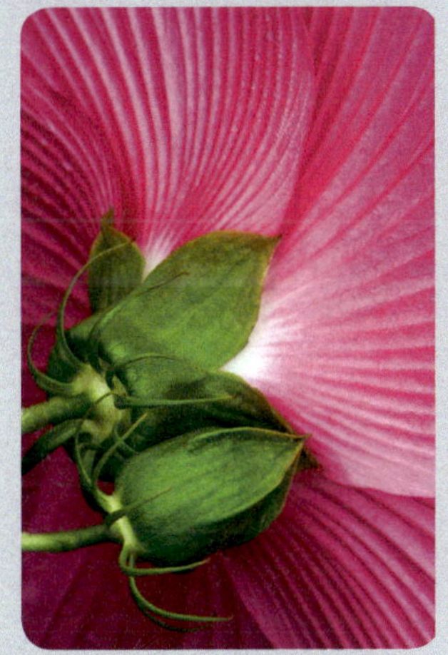

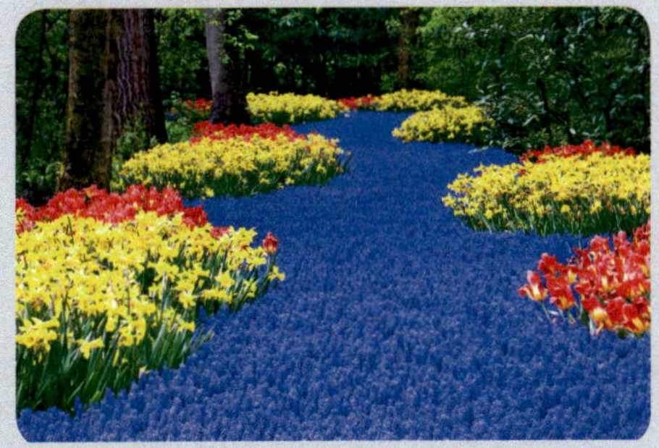

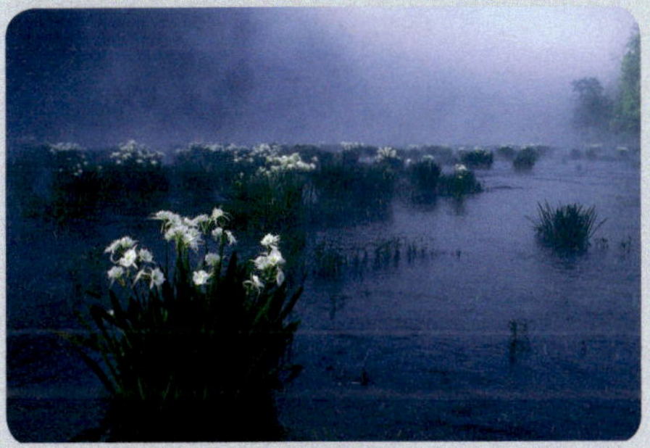

Clockwise from top left:

Grey-Headed Coneflowers, Daubenspeck Nature Park, Indianapolis, Indiana, *©Wendy Kaveney / Wendy Kaveney Photography*

Redwoods in the Fog, Redwoods National Park, California, *©Ronald Eberhart / Ron Eberhart Photography*

Pink Hibiscus Blossom, San Antonio Botanical Garden, Texas (Capt), *©Camille Lamoureux / Nims Images*

River of Blue, Keukenhof Gardens, Lisse, Holland, *©Charles Needle / Charles Needle Photography*

Cahaba Lilies in the Morning Mist, Cahaba River, Bibb County, Alabama, *©Beth Young*

FLORAL

Clockwise from top left:

Young Longleaf Regenerating in an Old Pine Forest, Wade Tract, Thomasville, Georgia, *©Beth Young*

Barred Owl with Crawfish, South Louisiana, *©Jude Haase*

Lupine Leaf, Raindrops, Waterloo Recreation Area, Michigan, *©Robert Domm / Robert Domm Photography*

Reeds Reflected in Pond, New Mexico, *©Andrea Sharon / LightPrints*

Windswept Grasses in the Craggy Gardens Area, Blue Ridge Parkway, North Carolina, *©Bill Gozansky / Bill Gozansky Photography*

LINED

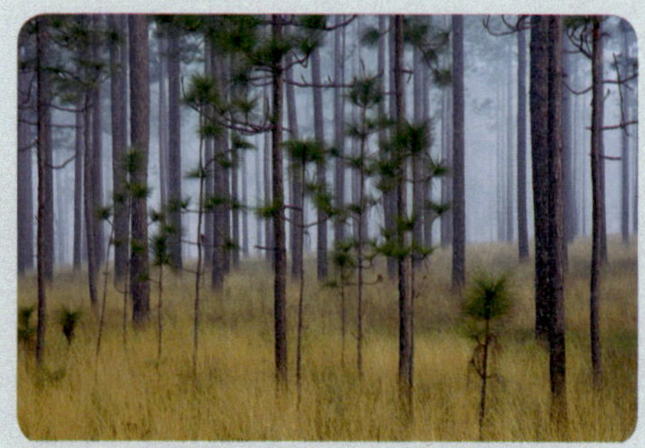

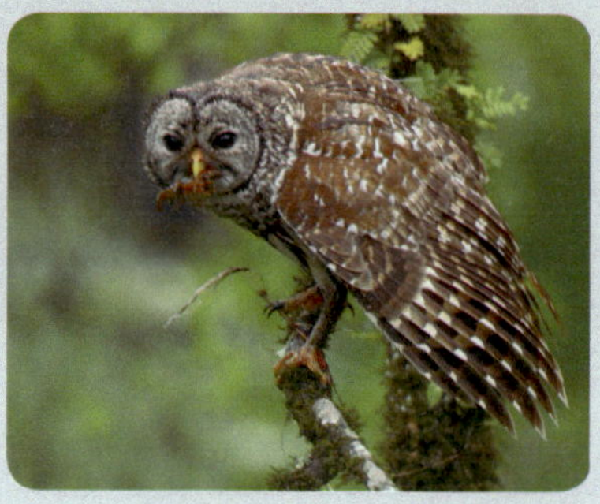

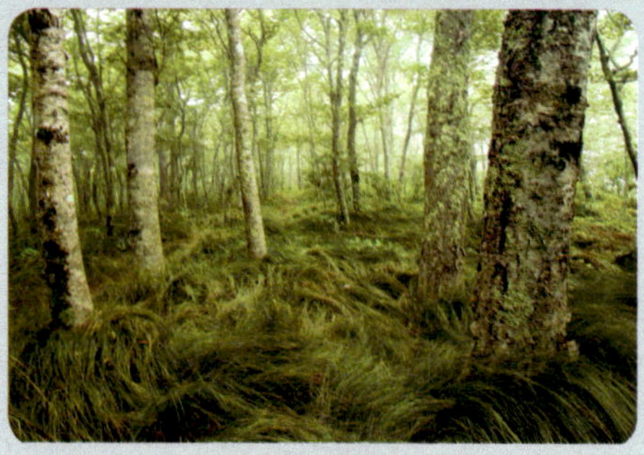

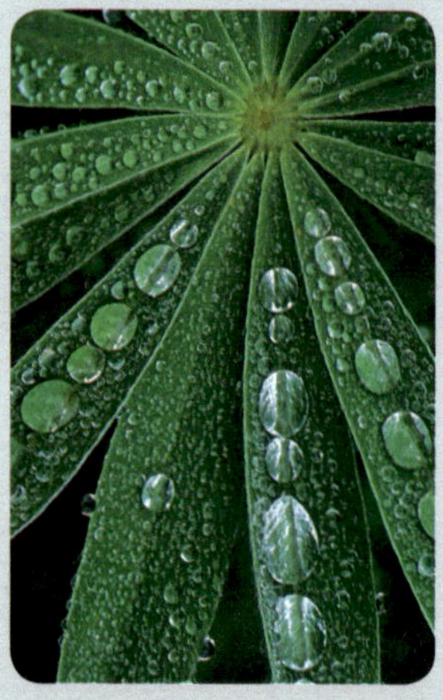

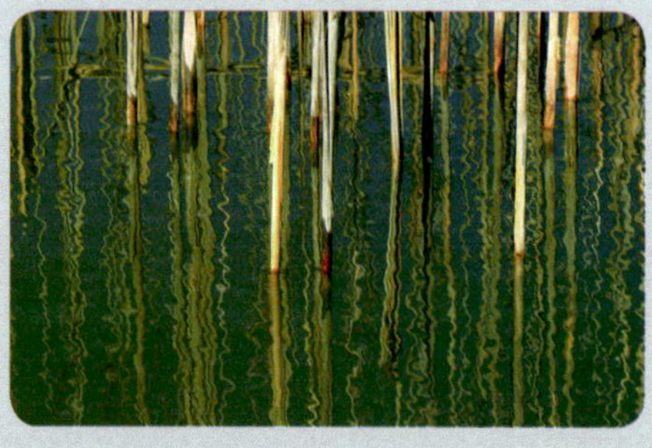

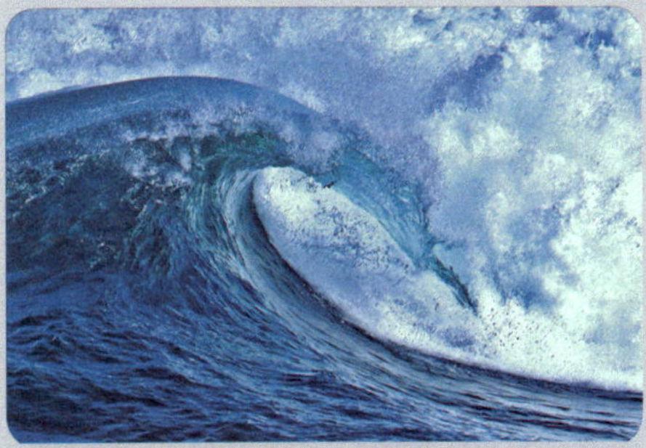

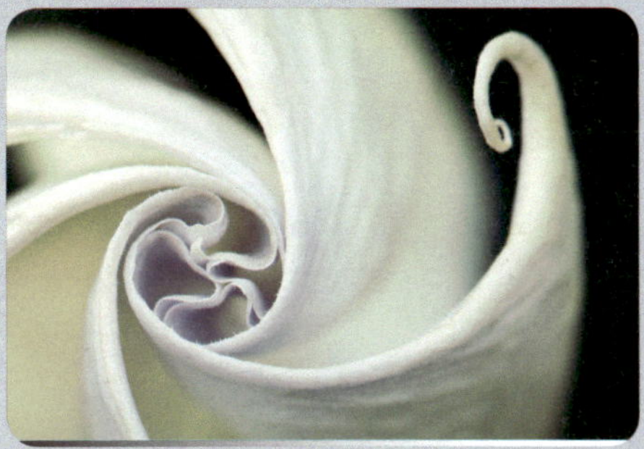

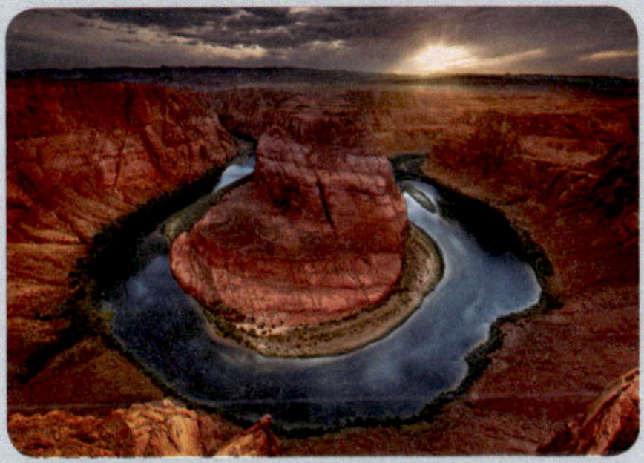

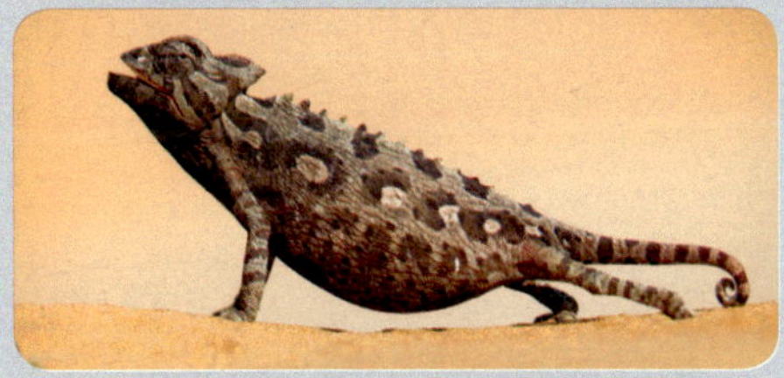

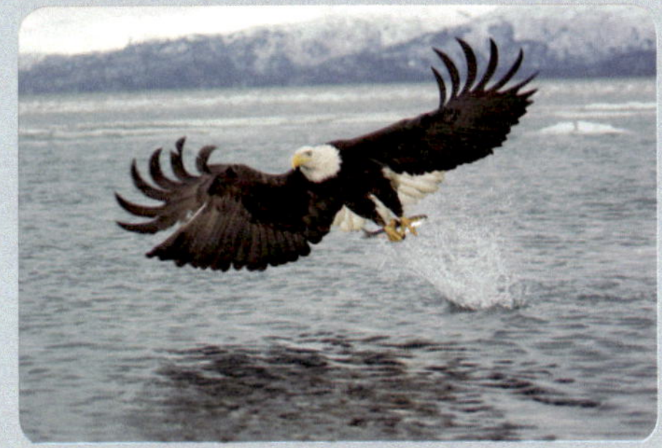

Clockwise from top left:

Wave Curl on the Coast of Depoe Bay, Oregon, *©Robert Petit*

Datura Pattern, Western Pennsylvania, *©Nancy Rotenberg / Natural Tapestries*

Namaqua Chameleon, Namib Desert, Namibia, *©Vida Ward / Vida Ward Photography*

Bald Eagle with Fish, Alaska, *©Timothy Mateer*

Turning Time, Canyon Edge, Horseshoe Bend, Arizona, *©Peter Lik*

CURL

Clockwise from top left:

Backyard Sunflower Reflections, Alpharetta, Georgia (Capt), *©Charles Needle / Charles Needle Photography*

Moon Jellyfish Swarm, Deep Bay, Baranof Island, Alaska, *©Ann Beisser*

Around the Campfire, Flat Tops Wilderness, Colorado, *©Michael Renner, Jr. / Timberline Images Photography*

Fall Color Reflection in Water Droplets, Ann Arbor, Michigan (Capt), *©Dietmar Haenchen*

Landscape Reflection in Soap Bubble, Amicalola Falls State Park, Georgia, *©George Bradfield / Through Nature's Eyes Photography*

ROUND

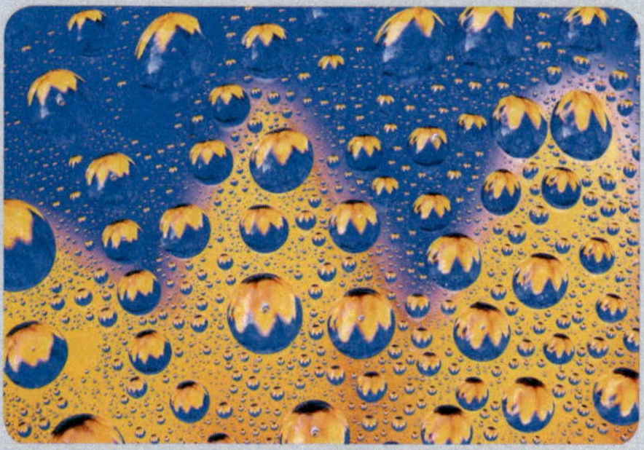

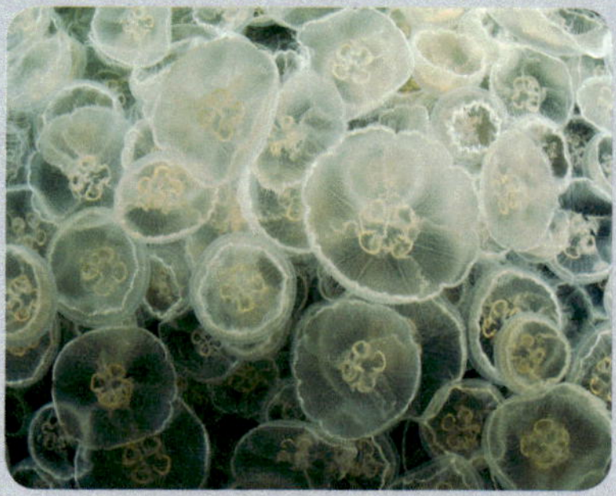

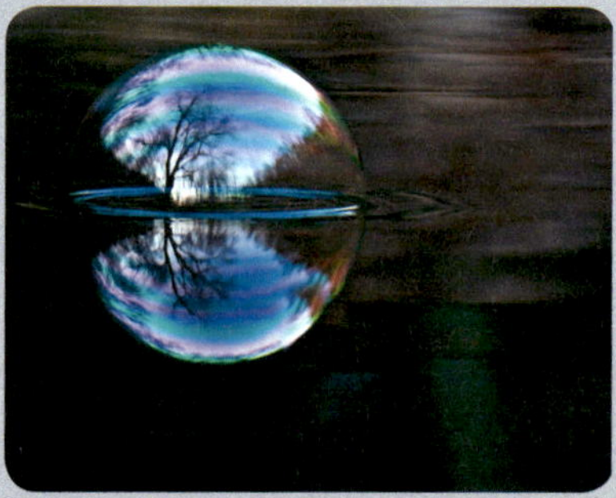

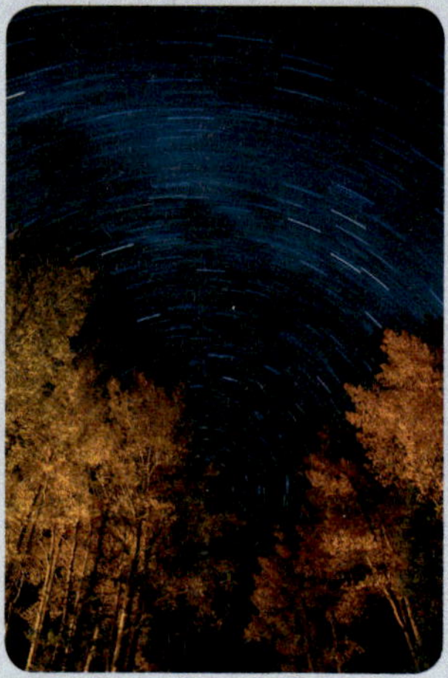

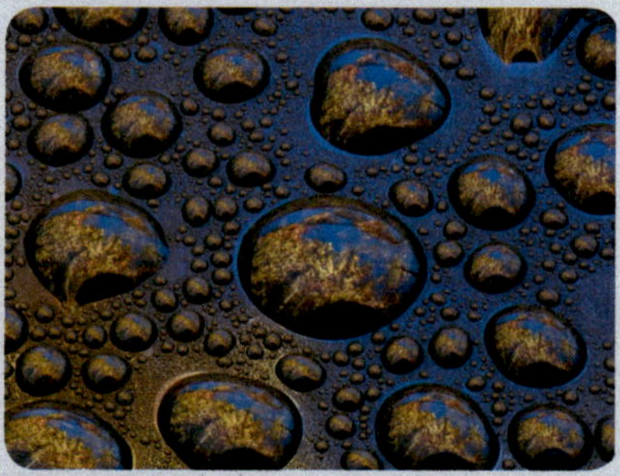

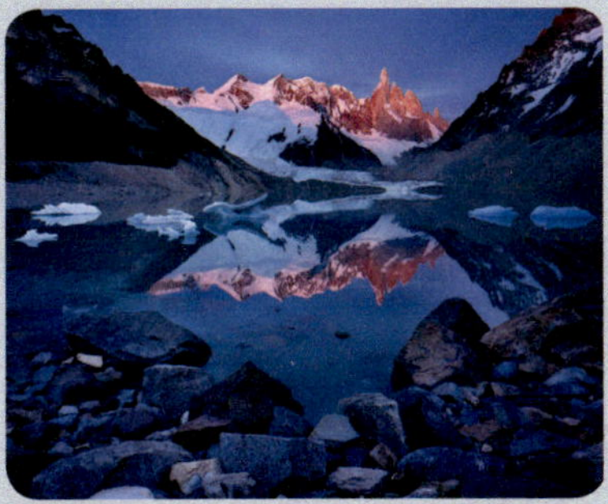

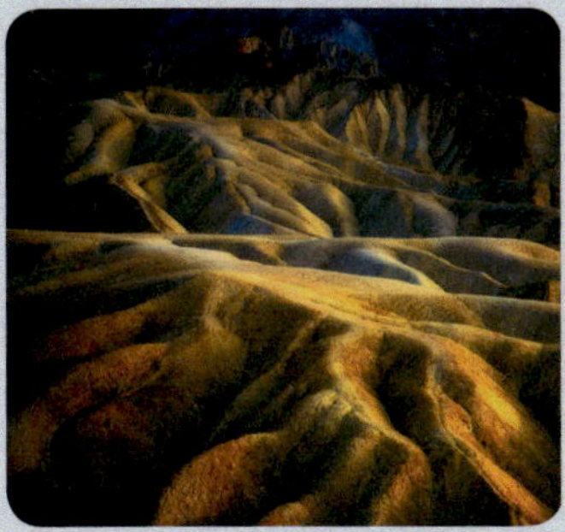

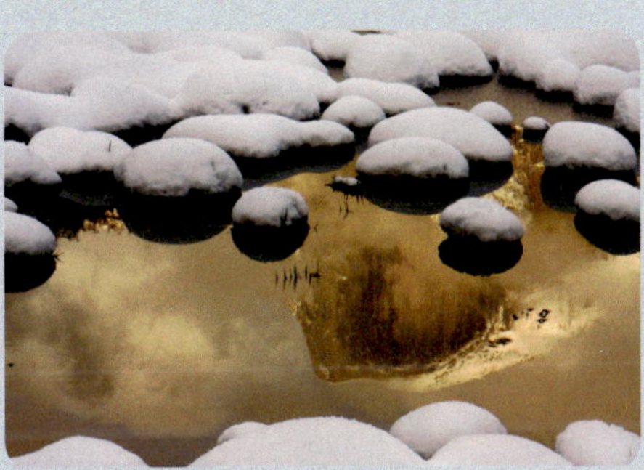

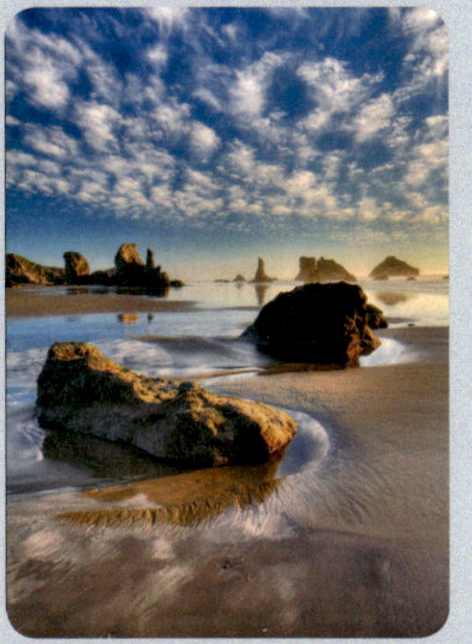

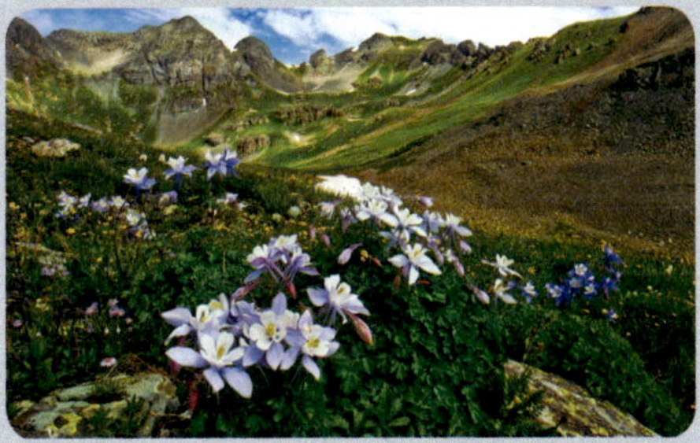

Clockwise from top left:

Cerro Torre Sunrise Reflection, Patagonia, Argentina, *©Jack Brauer / WideRange Photo LLC*

Desert Sandstorm at Zabriskie Point, Death Valley National Park, California, *©Trixi Huish / Trixi Huish Photography*

Sunset Dreamscape, Bandon, Oregon, *©Tim Lein / Tim Lein Photography*

Columbine Varieties, Colorado, *©Mike Walker*

Half Dome Reflection, Yosemite, California, *©Joseph Italiano*

ROCKY

Clockwise from top left:

A Tiny Landscape of Survival, Anza Borrego Desert, California, *©Jeffrey Sipress / Jeffrey Sipress Photography*

Morning Light on Wheatfields, The Palouse, Washington, *©Richard Duval / Duval Images*

Merced River Ice Flow, Merced River, Yosemite, California, *©Jay Hart*

A Hard Life, Arizona, *©Mark Lagrange*

Salt Tendrils, Namib Desert, Africa *©Vida Ward*

DIVIDED

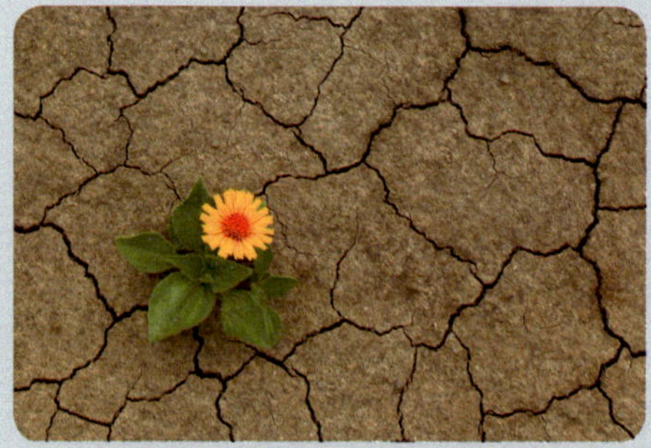

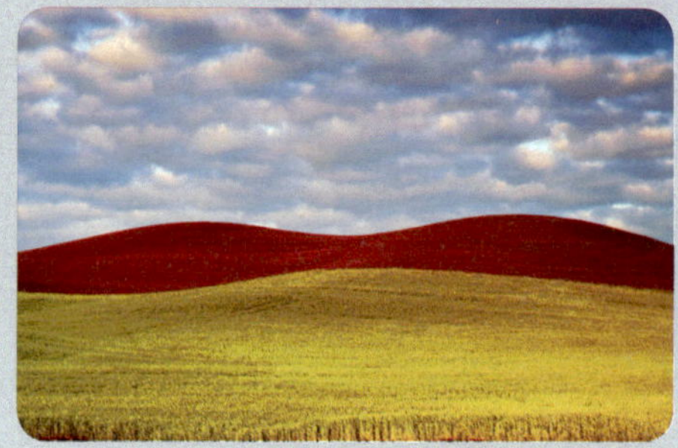

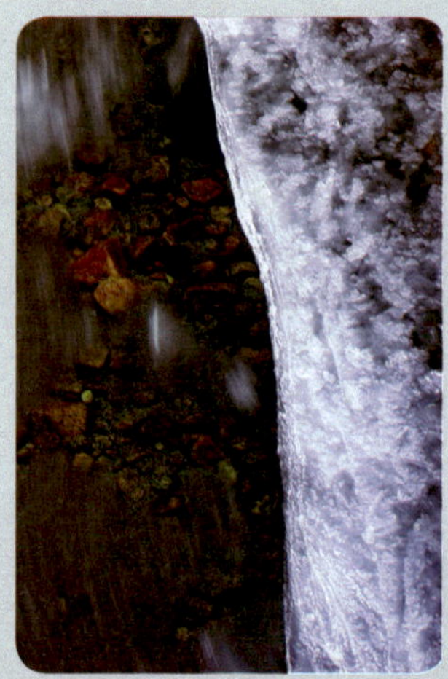

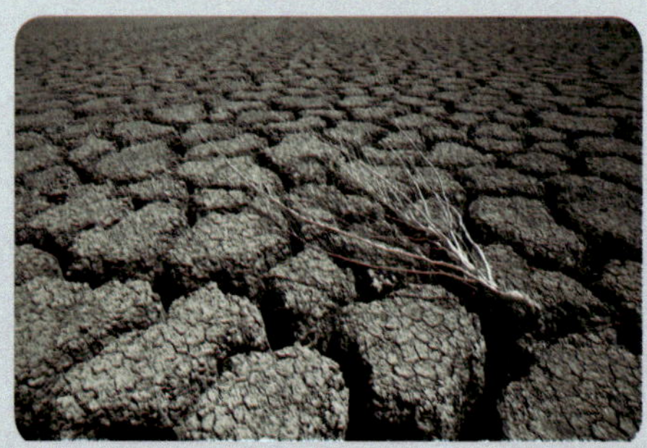

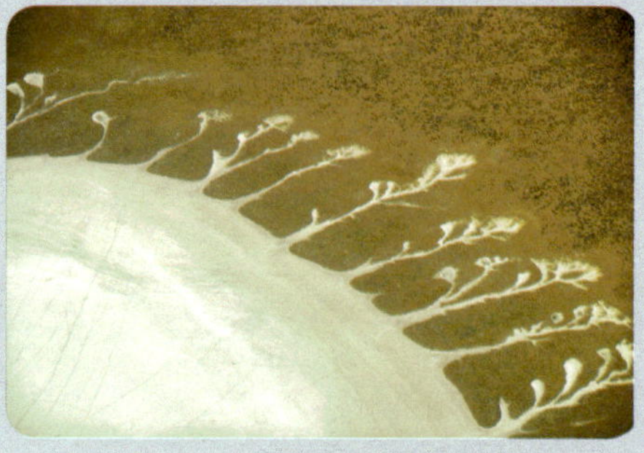

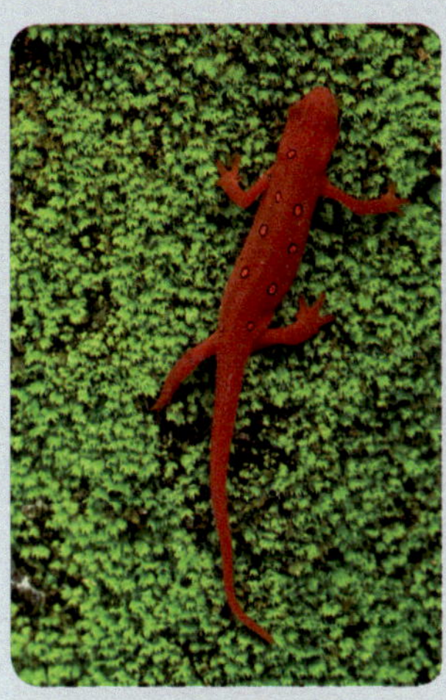

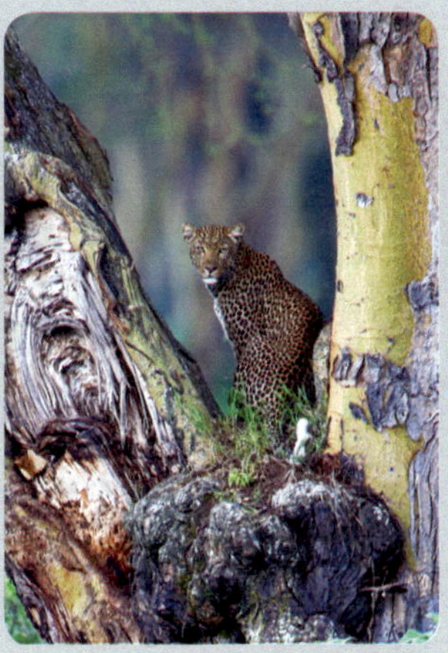

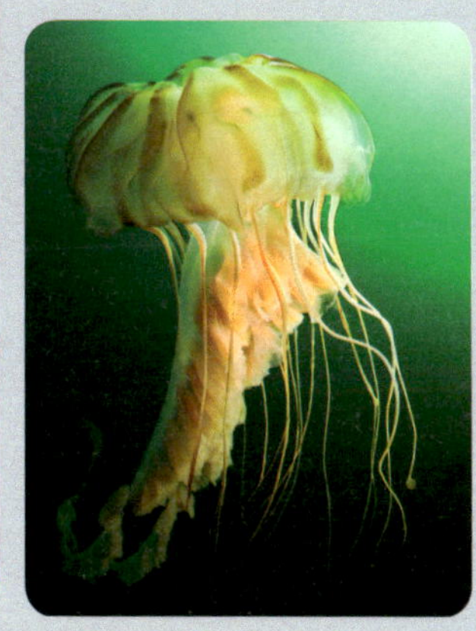

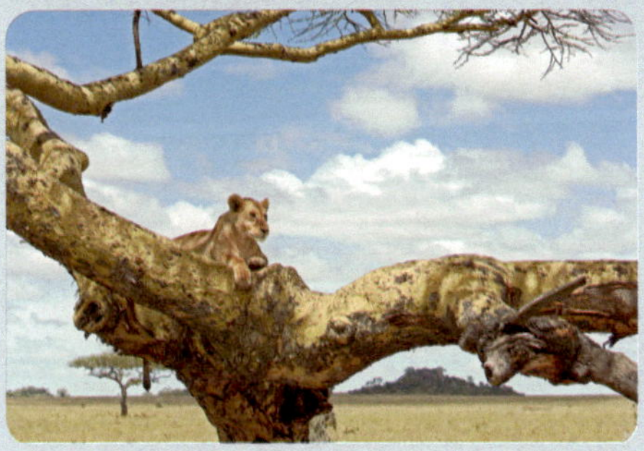

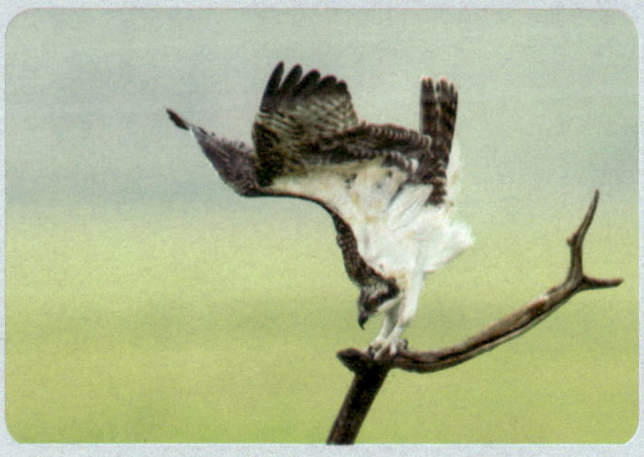

Clockwise from top left:

Red Eft, Cumberland Plateau, Tennessee, *©Bill Campbell / Bill Campbell Photography*

Leopard in a Tree, Africa, *©Joanne Williams / Joanne Williams Photography, Inc.*

Jellyfish, Deep Bay, Baranof Island, Alaska, *©Ann Beisser*

Osprey Wing Stretch, Long Island, New York, *©Thomas Pfeifer*

Lioness in Yellow-barked Acacia, Serengeti National Park, Tanzania, *©Bill Harbin*

UP

★★★TIER 3

★

★

WINNERS

Clockwise from top left:

Reflection of Clouds, Merritt Island National Wildlife Refuge, Florida, *©Robert Amoruso / Wildscape Images*

Sunrise Majestic, Glacier National Park, Montana, *©Sean Bagshaw / Outdoor Exposure Photography, LLC*

Early Morning at White Sands National Monument, New Mexico, *©Greg Ferguson / Greg Ferguson Photography*

Lightning Bolt, Rural Pulaski County, Illinois, *©David Hammond*

A Tree in Morning Fog, Marlinton, West Virginia, *©Jonathan Gordon*

CLOUDS

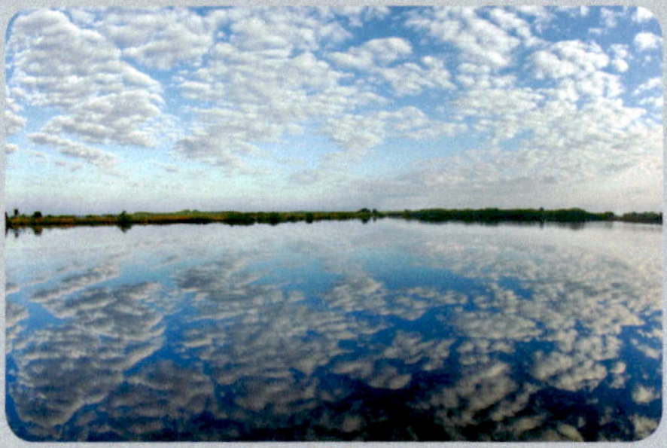

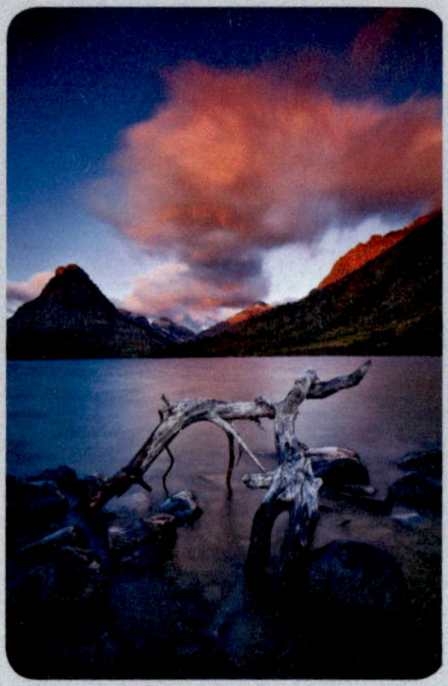

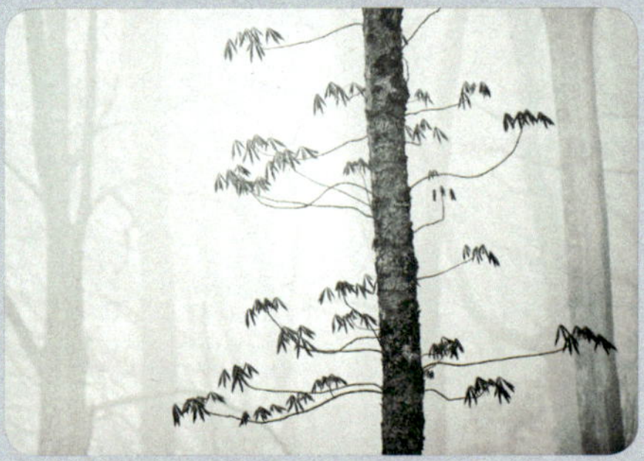

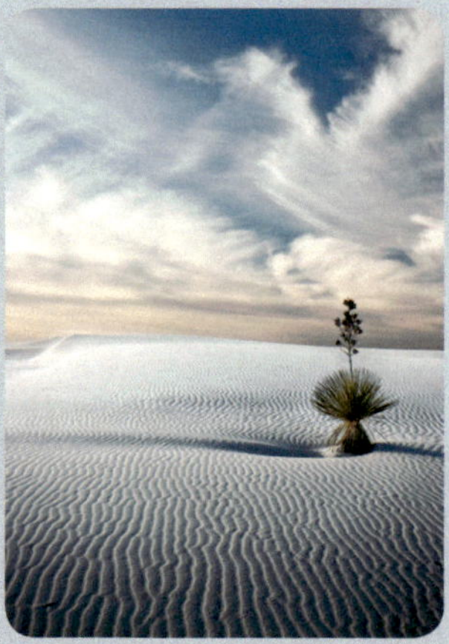

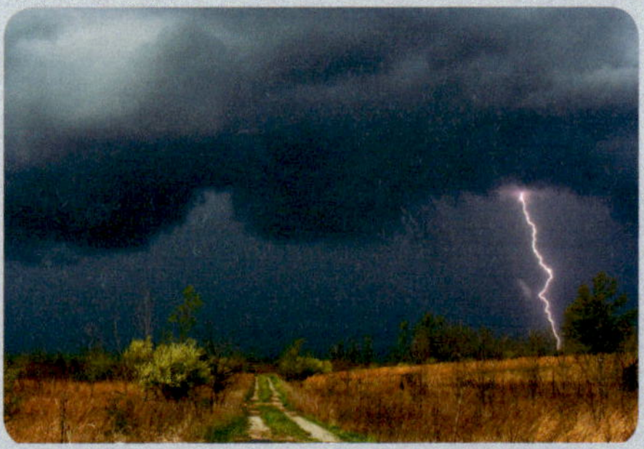

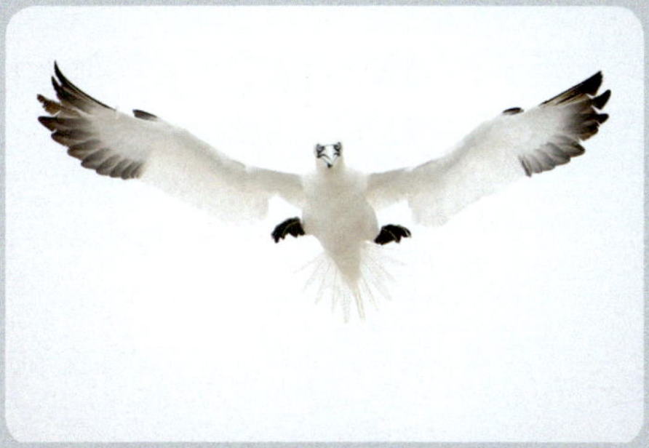

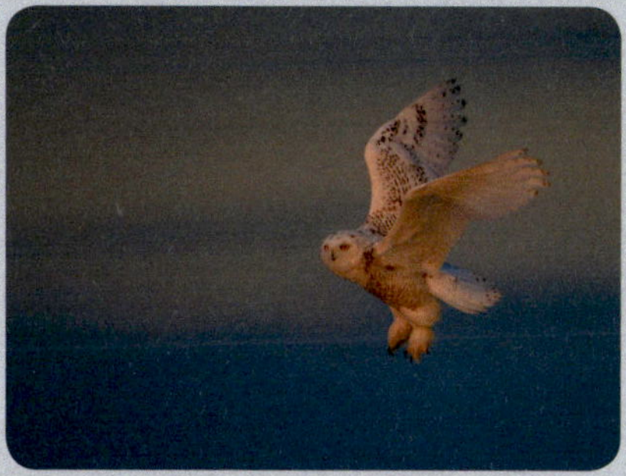

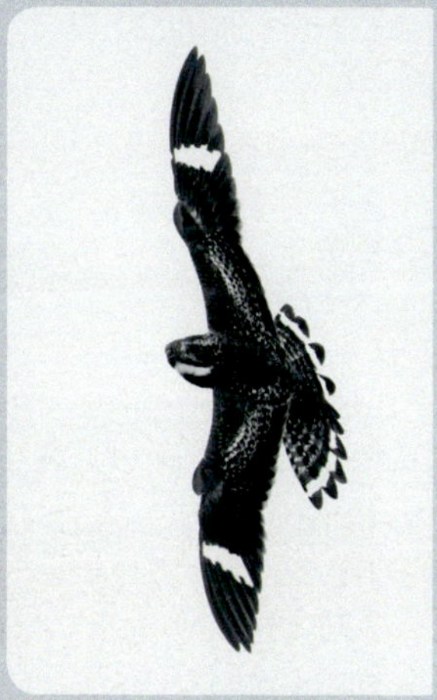

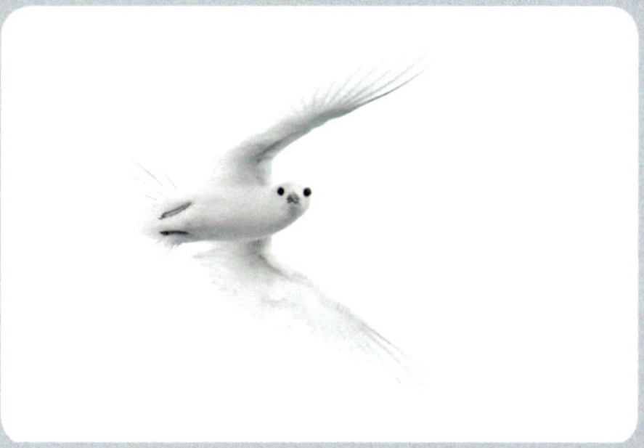

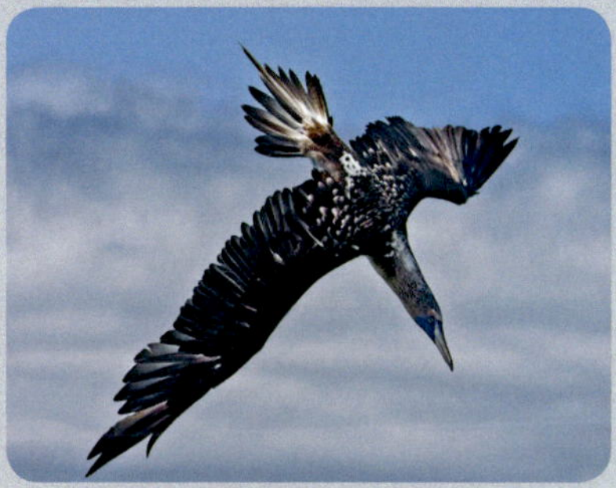

Clockwise from top left:

Northern Gannet, Bonaventure Island, Quebec, Canada, *©Michael Milicia / Michael Milicia Photography*

Snowy Owl, Jones Beach, New York, *©Bill Rudock*

Banked Turn of a Common Nighthawk, Big Cypress National Preserve, Florida, *©Kevin Barry*

White Tern, Midway Atoll, Hawaii, *©Daisy Gilardini*

Diving Blue-Footed Booby, Bartolomé Islands, Galapagos Island, Ecuador, *©David DesRochers*

FLIGHT

Clockwise from top left:

Snow Geese in Flight, Bosque del Apache National Wildlife Refuge, New Mexico, *©David Becker*

Geological Formation, Bryce Canyon National Park, Utah, *©Robert Dayton*

Moonlighting, Ecola State Park, Oregon, *©David Hutchison*

Sunset Trio Cheetahs, Masai Mara, Kenya, *©David Eicher / Dave Eicher Photography*

Iceberg, Jokulsarlon Glacial Lake, Iceland, *©Daisy Gilardini*

FORMATION

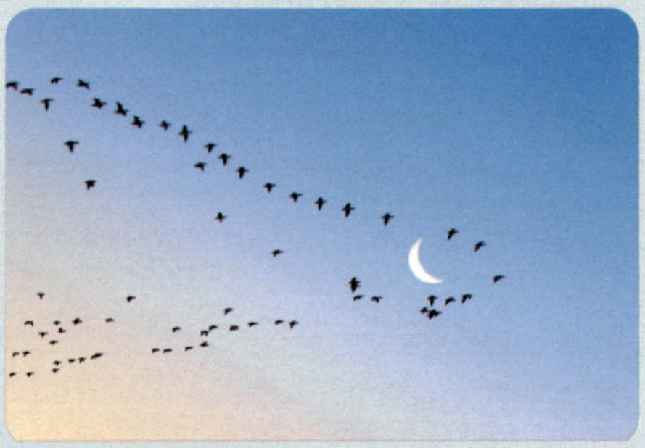

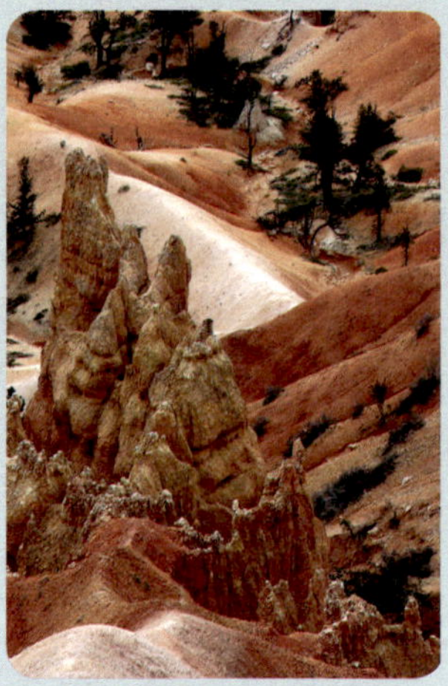

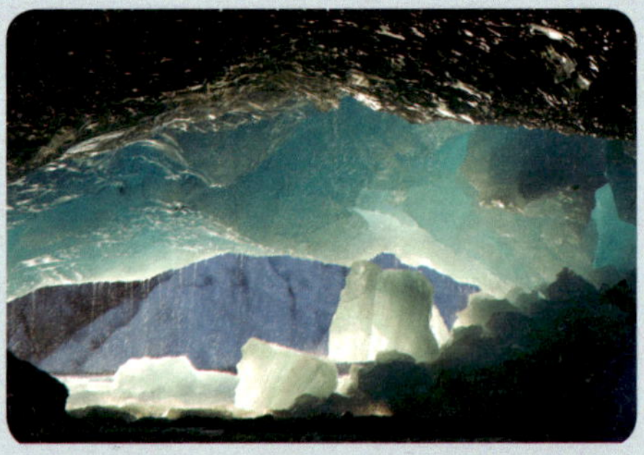

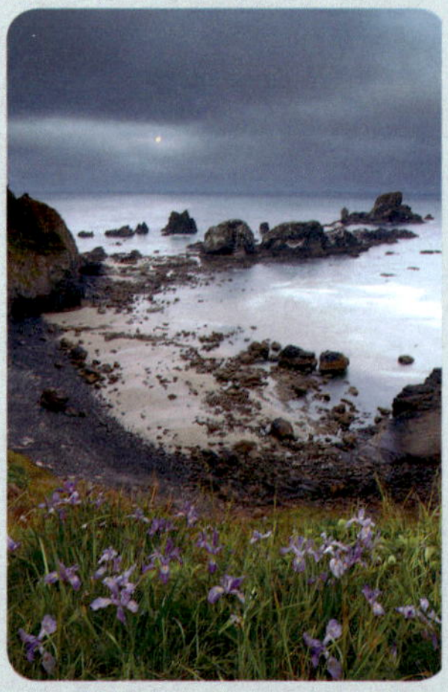

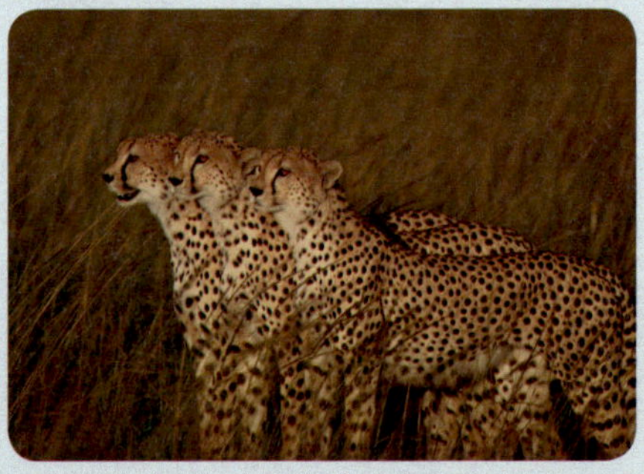

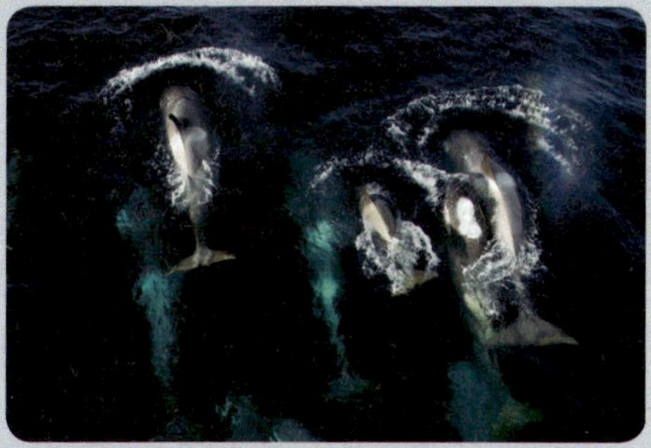

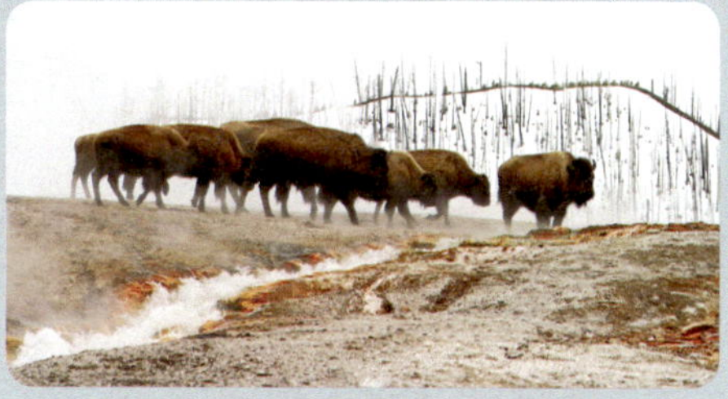

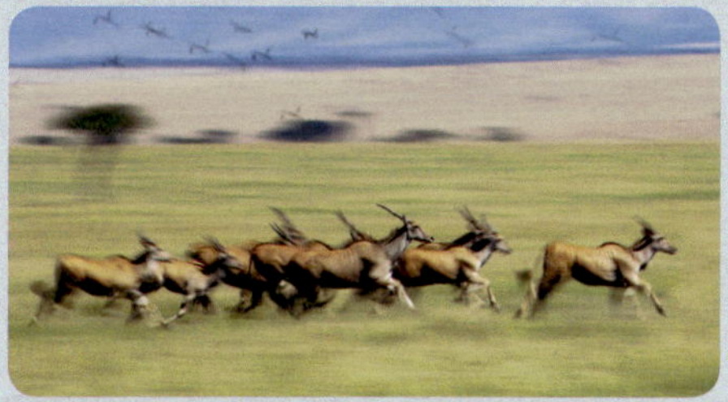

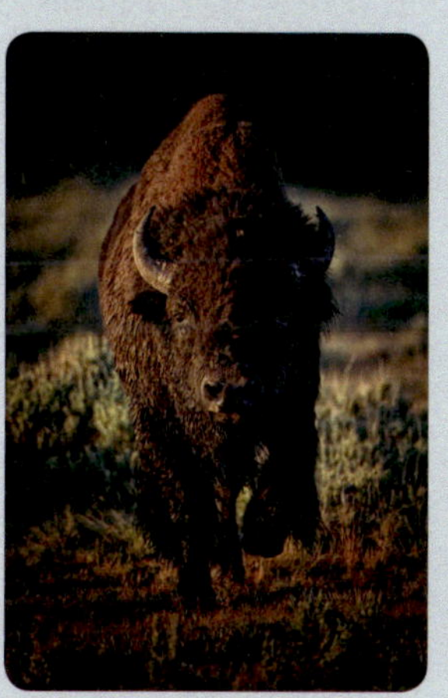

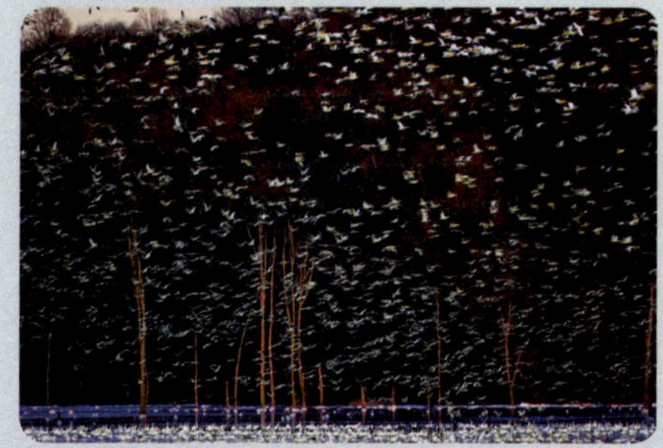

Clockwise from top left:

Pod of Orcas, Lemaire Channel, Antarctica, *©Charles Smith / Elk Meadow Images*

Bison Crossing Hot Spring Runoff, Yellowstone National Park, Wyoming, *©Thomas Stanton*

Charging Bull Buffalo During Fall Rut, Yellowstone National Park, Wyoming, *©Jeff Vanuga / Vanuga Photography*

Snow Geese Settling on Winter Lake at Sunset, Pennsylvania, *©Cliff Beittel*

Eland Herd on the Move, Serengeti National Park, Tanzania, *©Chris Gamel*

MOVING

Clockwise from top left:

Lightning Bug Takeoff, Richland County, Ohio (Capt), *©David FitzSimmons / FitzSimmons Photography*

Red Paper Wasp in Flight, Oklahoma, *©Ron Day / Ron Day Photography*

Kingfisher Shower, Chincoteague National Wildlife Refuge, Virginia, *©Patrick Lynch / Images Unlimited*

Osprey with Mackerel, Southwest Florida, *©Lorraine Thomas*

Barn Owl, Utah (Phil), *©Douglas Brown / BirdWhisperer Photography*

FLY

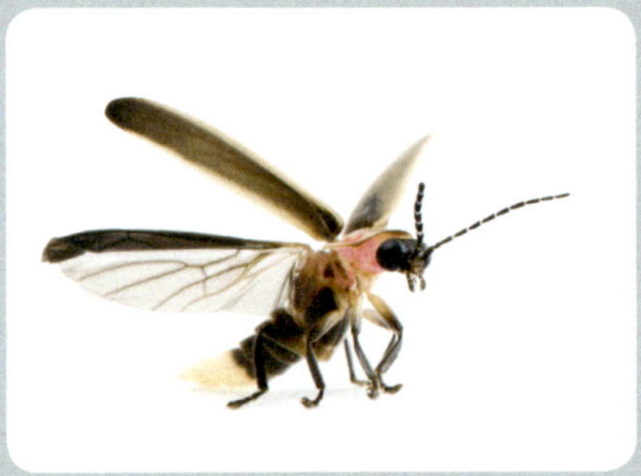

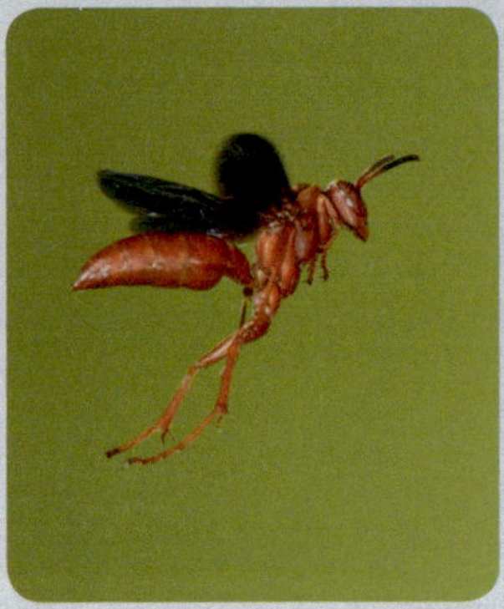

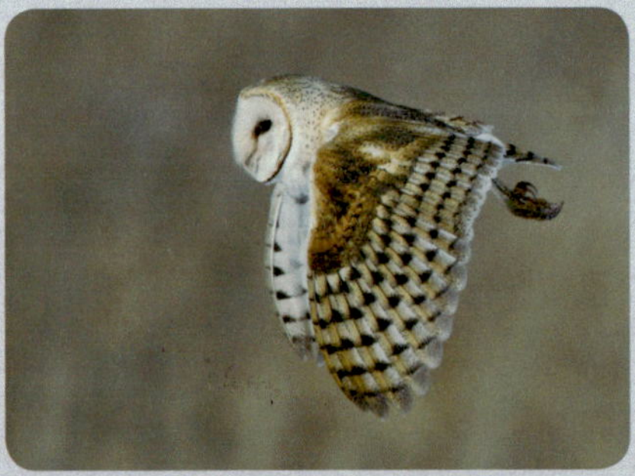

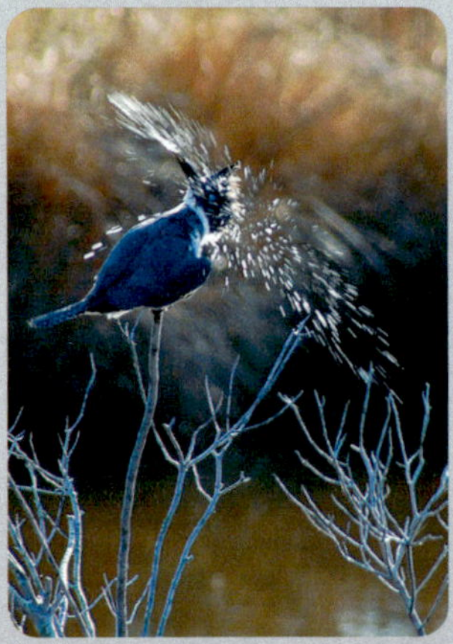

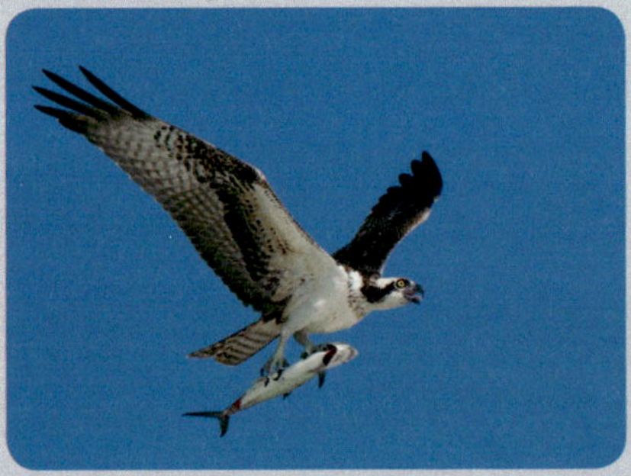

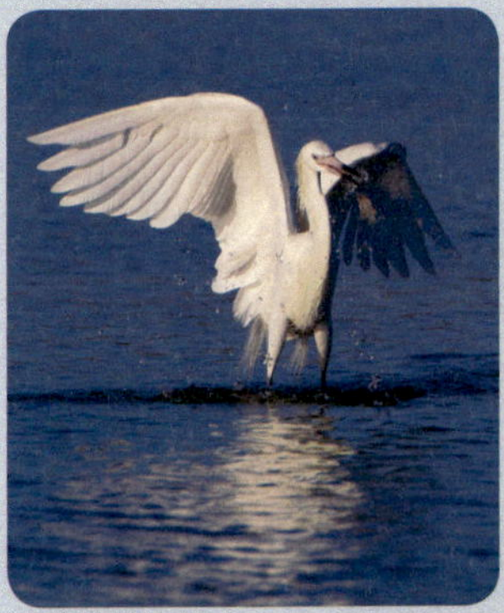
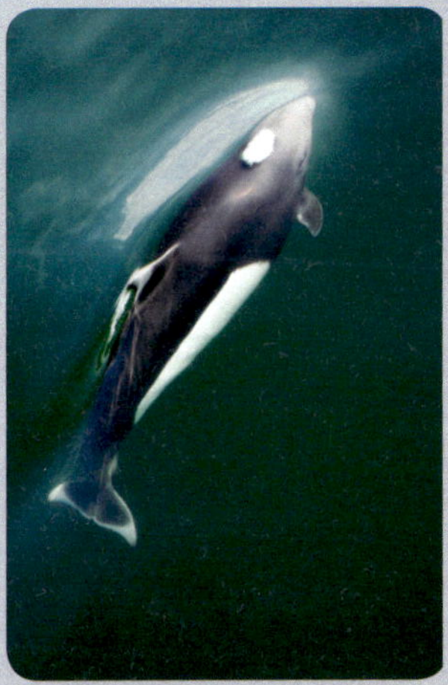
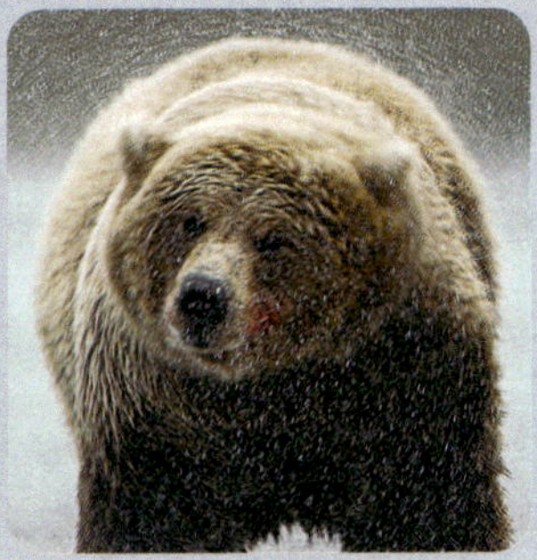
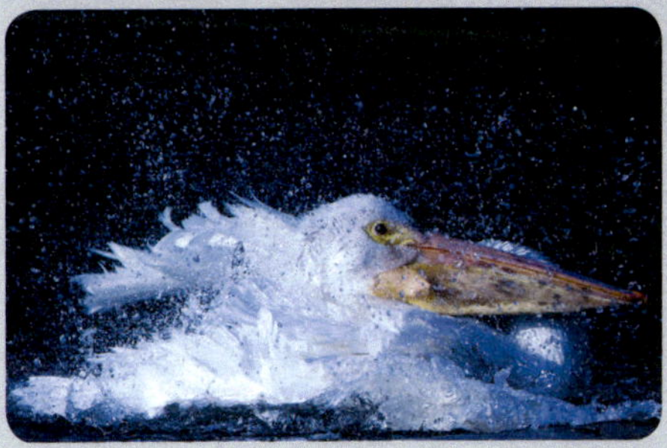
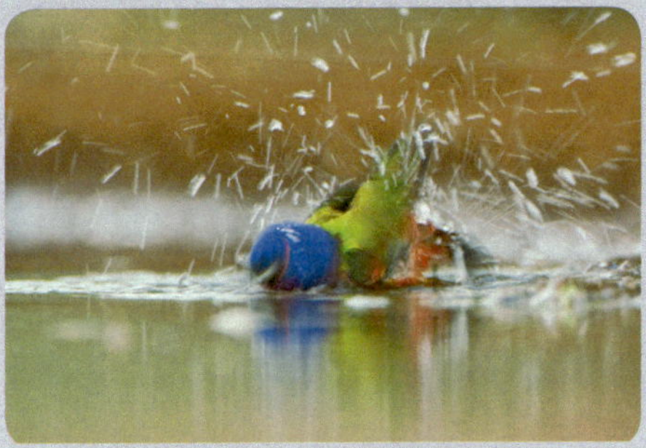

Clockwise from top left:

Reddish Egret Catching Fish, Ft. De Soto County Park, Florida, *©Don Saunders / Don Saunders Photography*

Dall's Porpoise, Southeast Alaska, *©Amy Gulick / Amy Gulick Photography*

Coastal Brown Bear, Lake Clark National Park, Alaska, *©Jim Mitchell*

Water Dance, Painted Bunting Bathing, Rio Grande Valley, Texas, *©Rob Tilley / Rob Tilley Photography*

White Pelican, White Rock Lake, Dallas, Texas, *©Jim Mitchell*

SPLASH

Clockwise from top left:

Moment of Kill, Coyote and Bison Calf in Yellowstone National Park, Lamar Valley, Wyoming, *©Mark Lagrange*

Fighting Zebras, Ngorongoro Crater, Tanzania, *©Keith Kennedy*

Bighorn Leaping onto the Back of Another, Yellowstone National Park, Montana, *©Thomas Stanton*

Polar Bear with Ringed Seal Prey, High Arctic, Russia, *©Sue Flood / Tartan Dragon Ltd*

Polar Bears, Cape Churchill, Canada, *©Antonio Visiola*

ATTACK

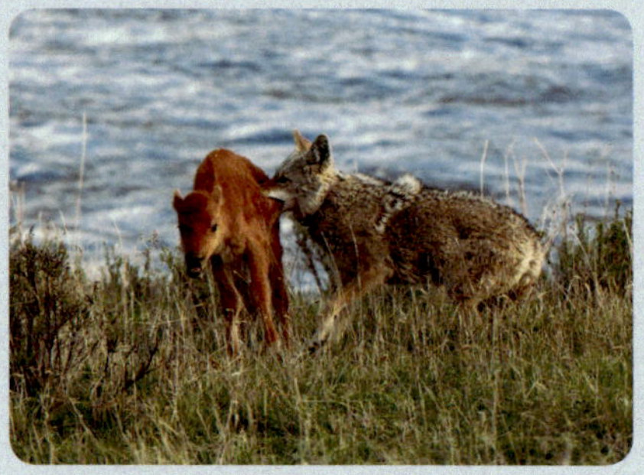

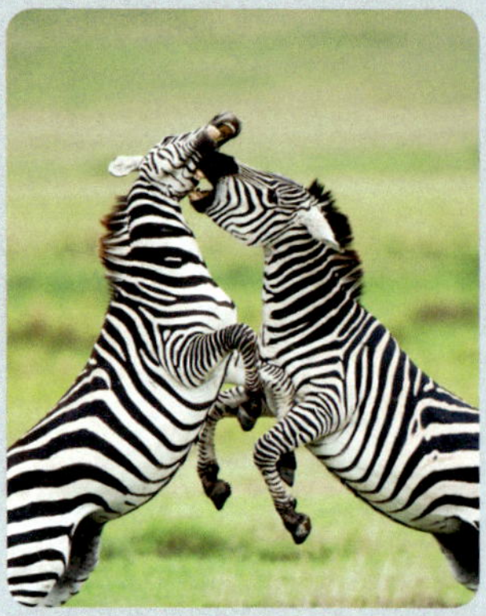

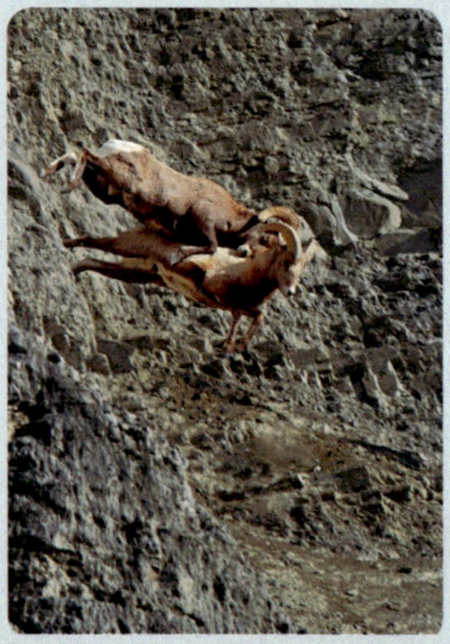

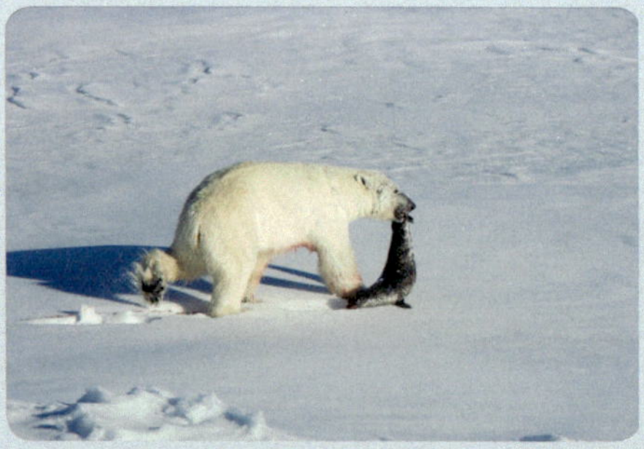

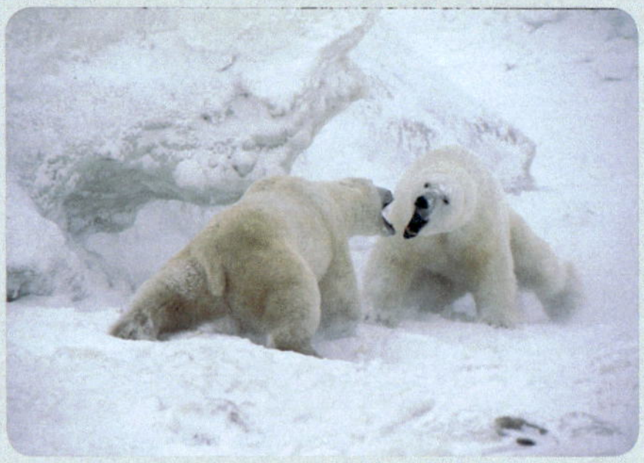

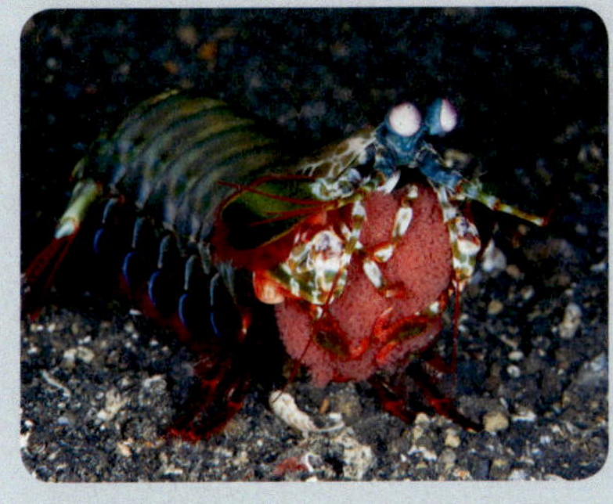

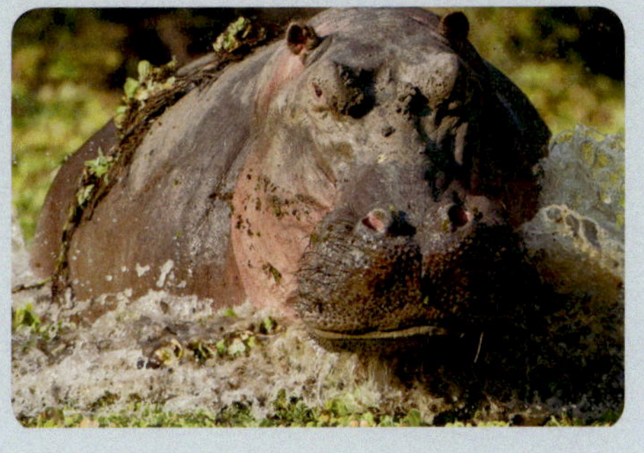

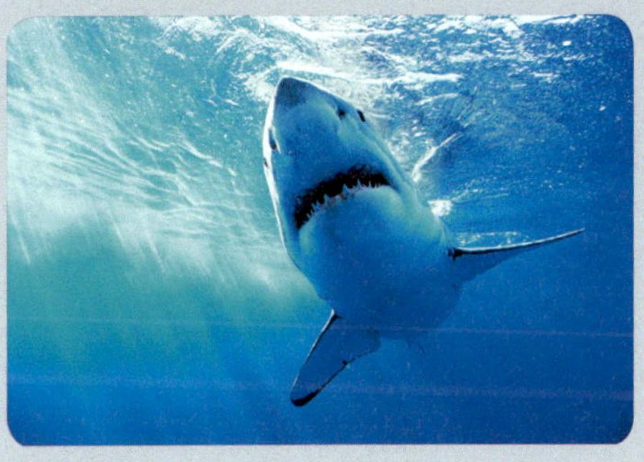

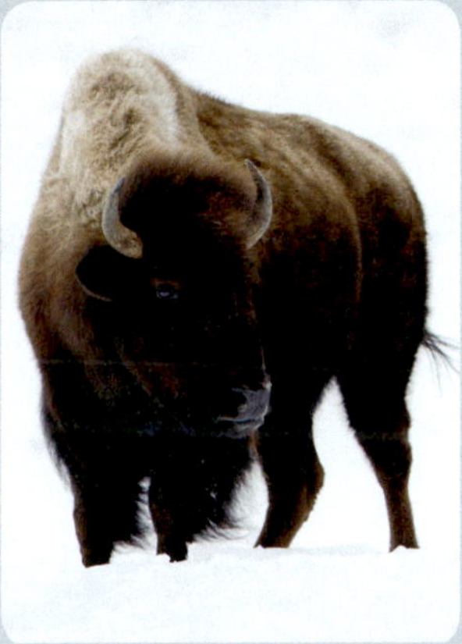

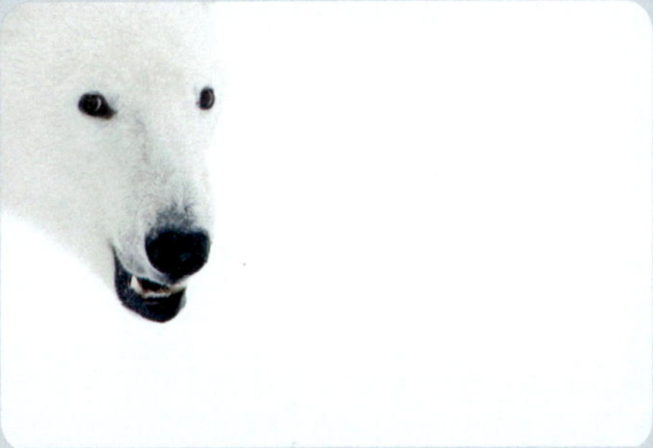

Clockwise from top left:

Mantis Shrimp Carrying Egg Mass, Lembeh Strait, North Sulawesi, Indonesia, *©Christopher Crowley*

Hippo Charge, South Luangwa National Park, Zambia, *©Gero Heine / Gero Heine Photography*

Bison, Yellowstone National Park, Wyoming, *©Gero Heine / Gero Heine Photography*

Polar Bear, Wapusk National Park, Canada, *©Daisy Gilardini*

Great White Shark, Guadalupe Island, Mexico, *©Sue Flood / Tartan Dragon Ltd*

POWER

Clockwise from top left:

Black Vulture on the Beach, Fort Myers Beach, Florida, *©Daniel Cedras*

Nudibranch, Dumaguete, Philippines, *©Ricky Ferguson / Fotos N Fins*

Greater Prairie Chickens in Battle, Dexter, Kansas, *©Greg Lasley*

Snowy Egret, Fort Myers Beach, Florida, *©Adams Serra*

Sandhill Cranes Landing at Dusk, Bosque del Apache National Wildlife Refuge, New Mexico, *©Stephen Weaver / Earth Systems Imaging*

CONFIDENT

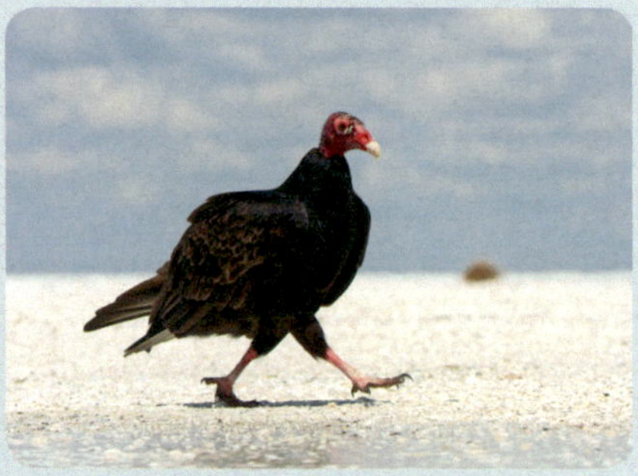

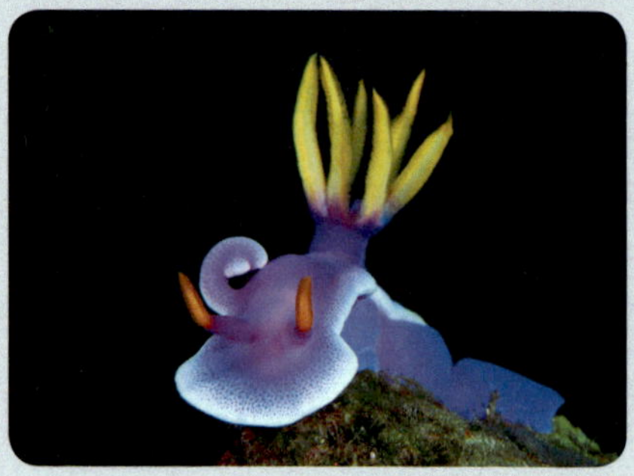

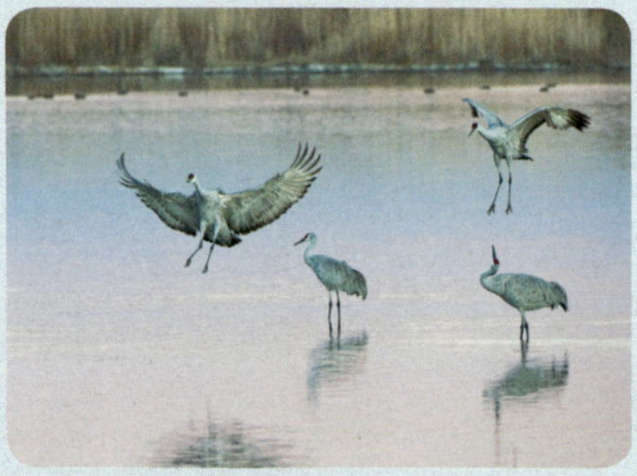

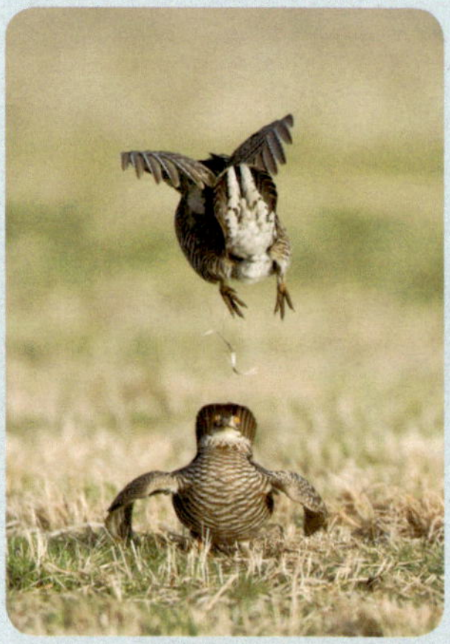

JUDGE'S CHOICE

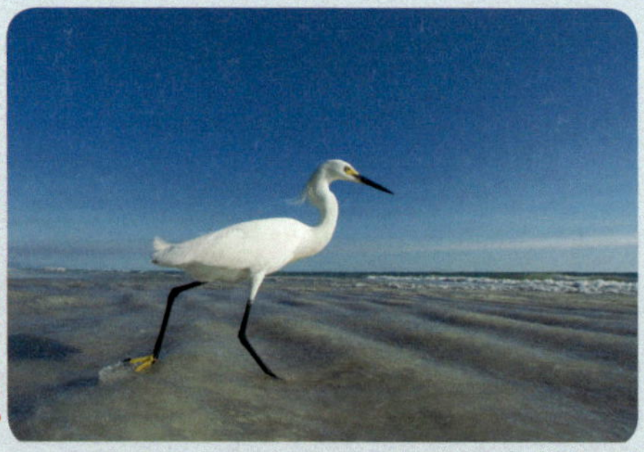

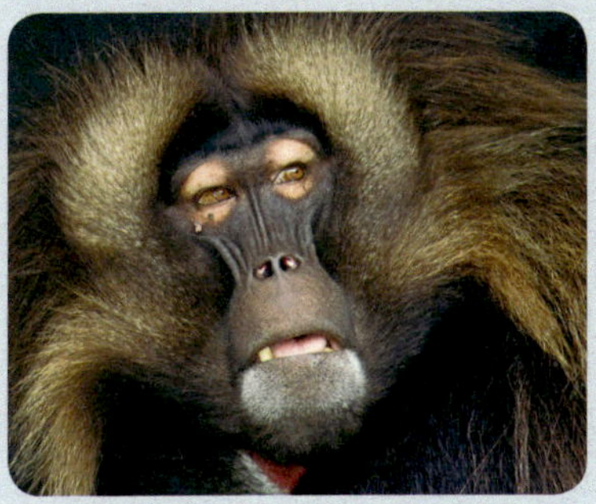

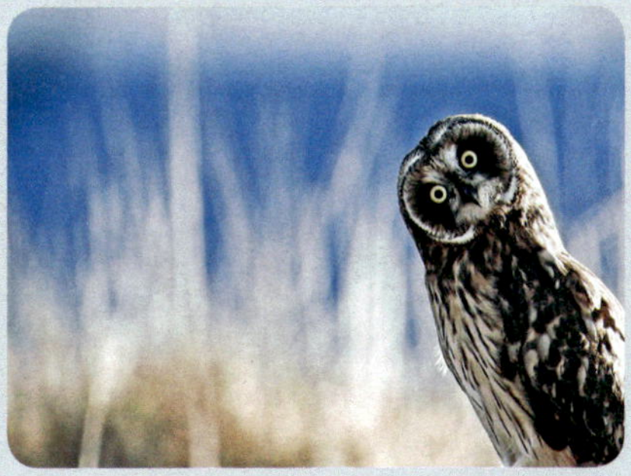

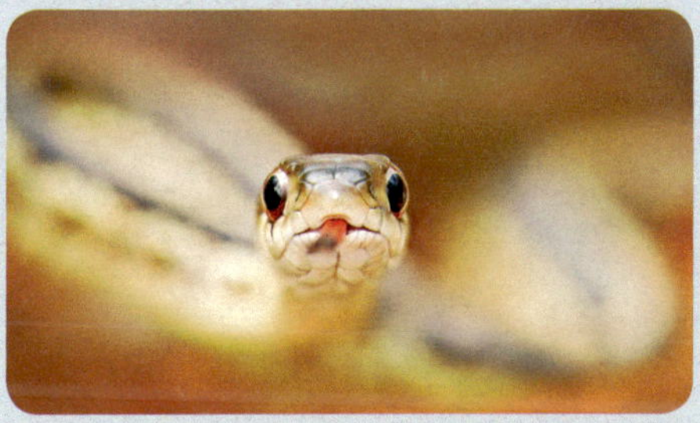

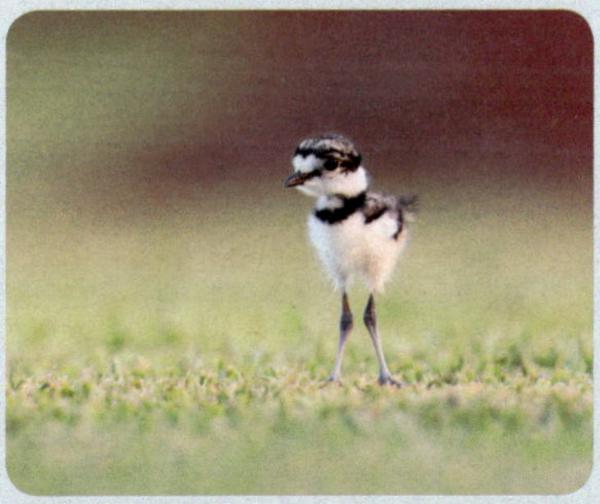

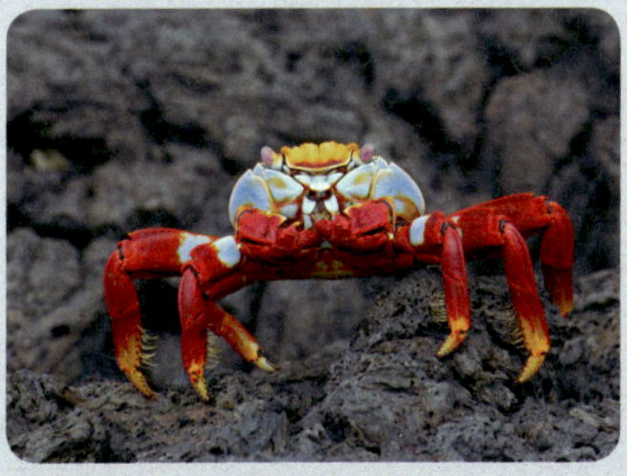

Clockwise from top left:

Gelada Baboon, Bronx Zoo, New York (Capt), *©David DesRochers*

Pue'o (Short-eared Owl), Slopes of Mauna Kea, Hawaii, *©Dwayne Longenbaugh*

Eastern Garter Snake, Bernardsville, New Jersey, *©Jim Gilbert*

Baby Killdeer, South Louisiana, *©Jude Haase*

Sally Lightfoot Crab, Santiago Island, Galapagos Islands, Ecuador, *©Donna Carr*

CURIOUS

Clockwise from top left:

Mating Elephant Seals and Pup, Piedras Blancas, California, *©Roberta Olenick / Never Spook the Animals Wildlife Photography*

Gambel's Quail Argument, Elephant Head, Arizona, *©Nathan Chappell / Trogon Tours, Inc.*

Elk Fight, Rocky Mountain National Park, Colorado, *©Thomas Wood*

Coastal Brown Bear Sow and Cub, Lake Clark National Park, Alaska, *©Robert Amoruso / Wildscape Images*

Bald Eagle Stare Down, Haines, Alaska, *©Mark Lissick / Wildlight Nature Photography*

ENGAGE

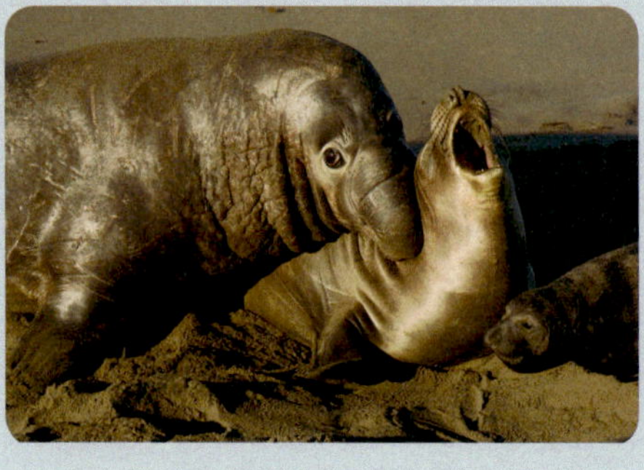

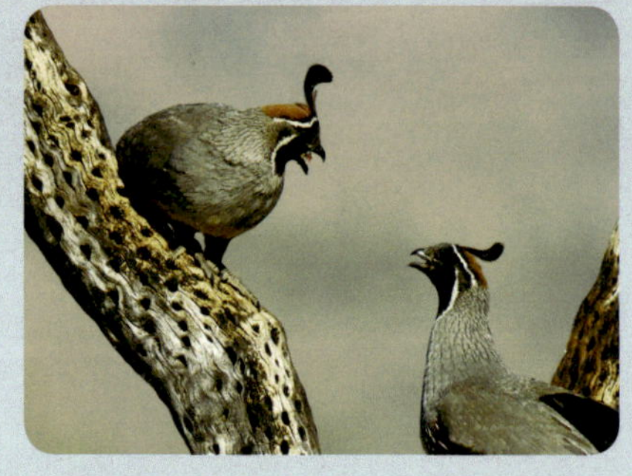

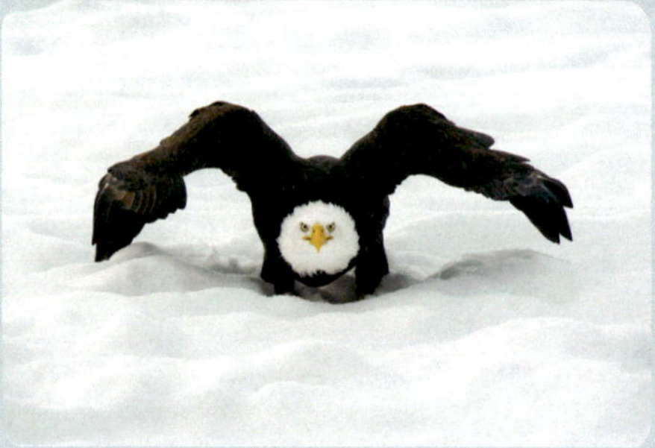

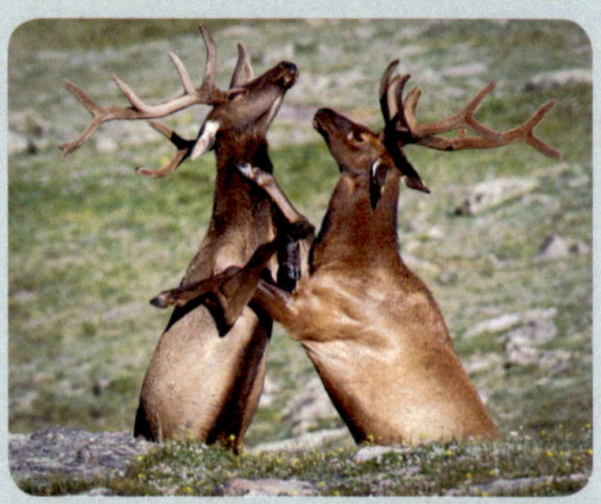

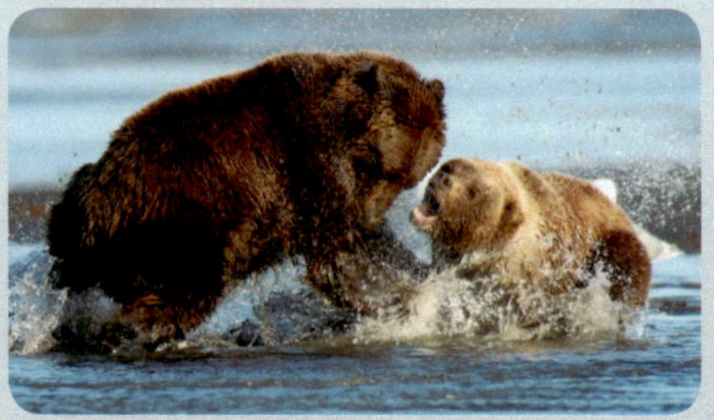

JUDGE'S CHOICE

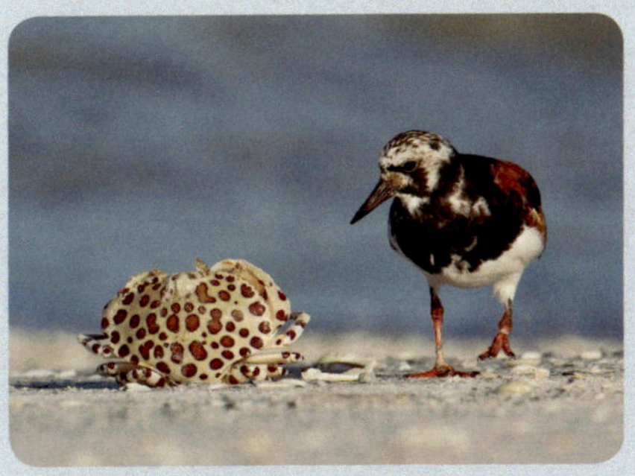

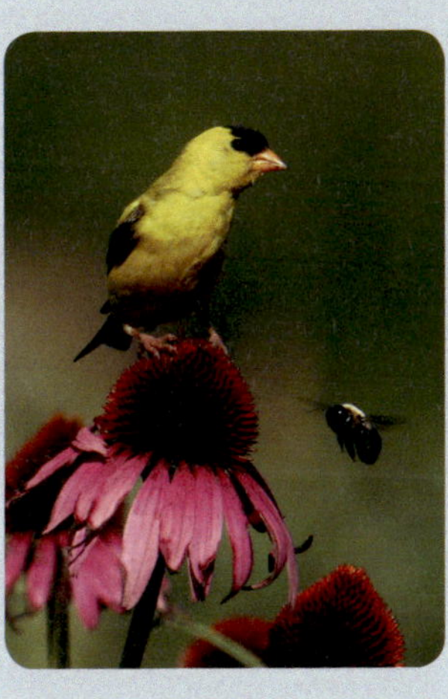

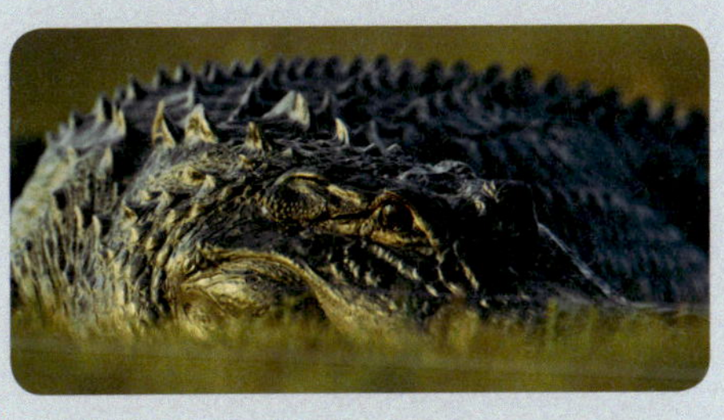

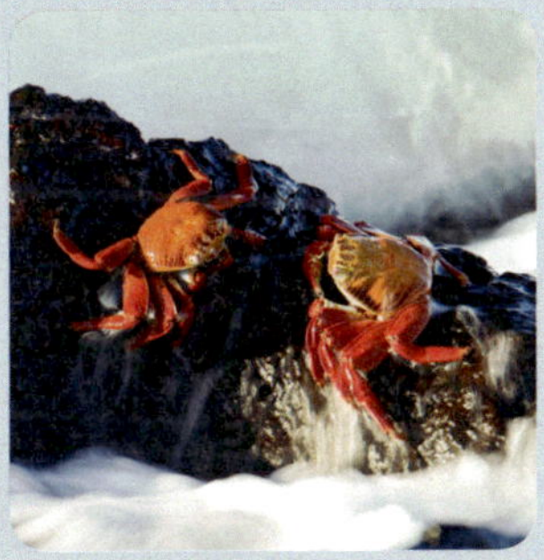

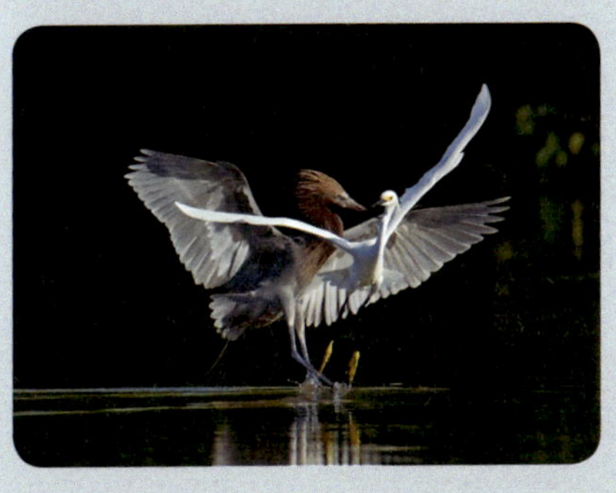

Clockwise from top left:

Ruddy Turnstone Attacking Leopard Crab, Ft. De Soto County Park, Florida, *©Don Saunders / Don Saunders Photography*

Goldfinch & Bee, Chicago Botanic Garden, Glencoe, Illinois, *©Jacqueline Tilles*

Sally Lightfoot Crabs in Surf, Galapagos Islands, Ecuador, *©Michael Henry*

Egret Lake, J. N. Ding Darling National Wildlife Refuge, Sanibel Island, Florida, *©Geoff Coe / Wild Images Florida*

Alligator in Warm Light, Viera, Florida, *©Shawn Marques / Shoot To Thrill Images*

MEET WINNERS

TIER 3 ★★★

Clockwise from top left:

Bear with Salmon, Brooks Falls, Katmai National Park, Alaska, *©Roman Kurywczak / Roamin with Roman Photo Tours*

Roadrunner with Lizard Prey, Hidalgo County, Texas, *©Cathy Illg / Adventure Photography*

Assassin Bug with Prey, Fruit & Spice Park, Miami, Florida, *©Alfred Forns*

Black Skimmer Chick with Eyes Bigger than Stomach, Pinellas County, Florida, *©Marina Scarr*

American Coot Parent and Juvenile, Santee, California, *©Diane Johnson / Diane Johnson Photography*

CONSUME

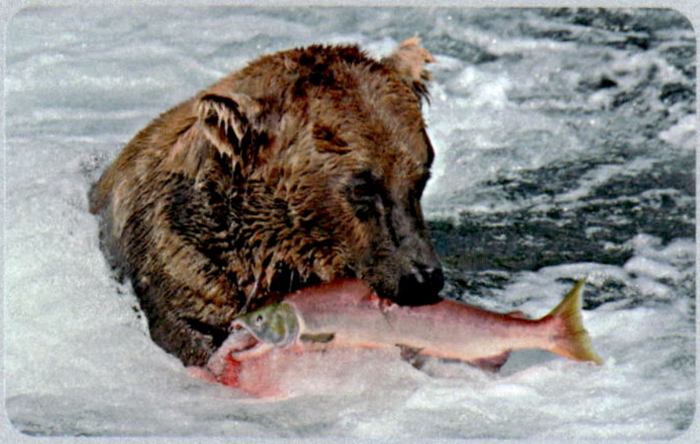

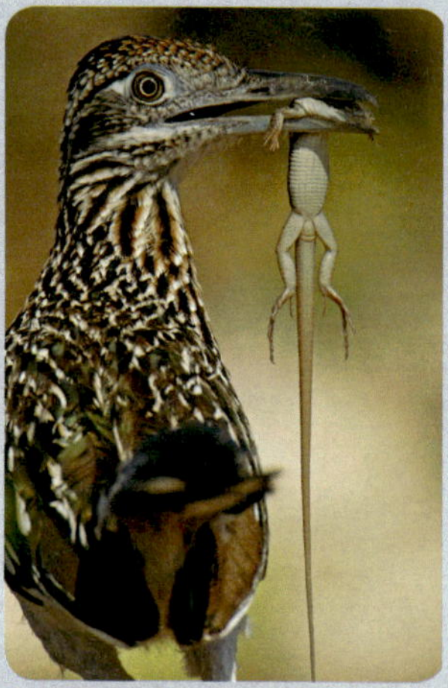

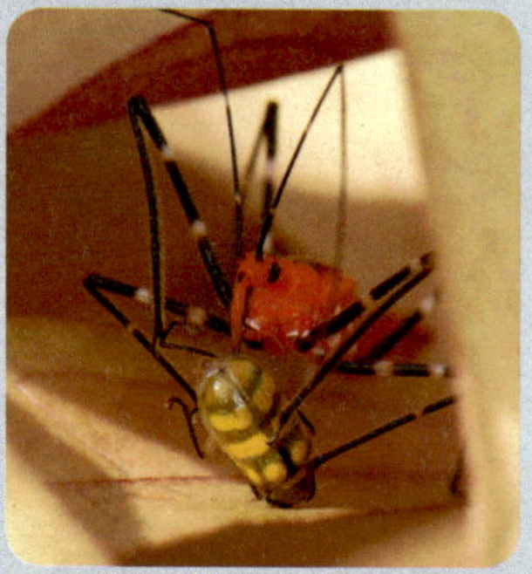

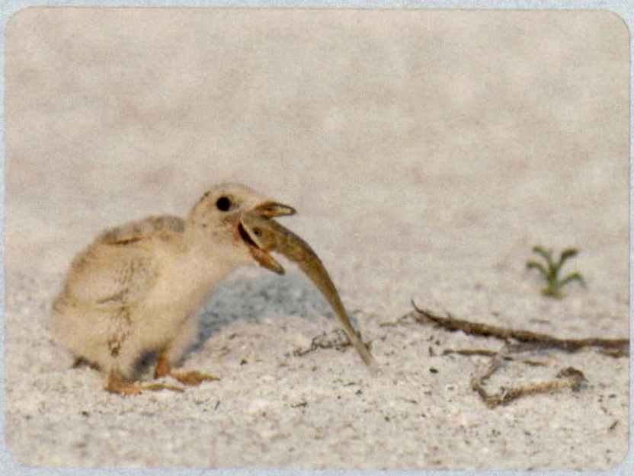

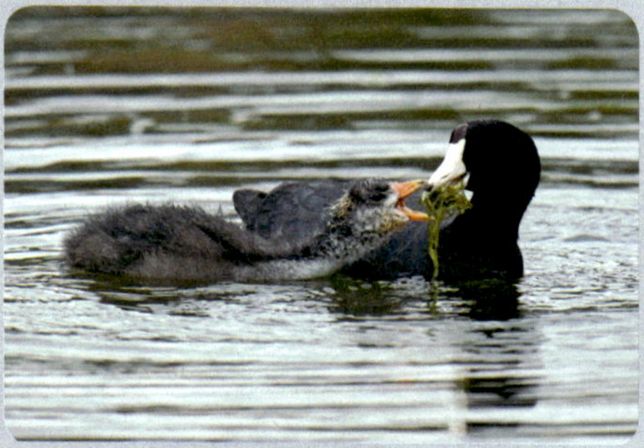

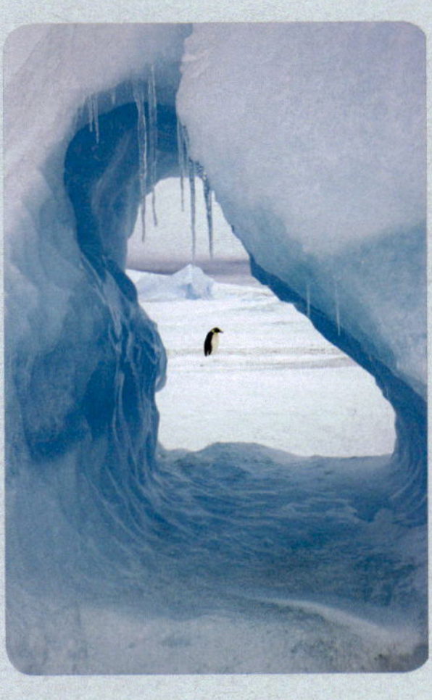

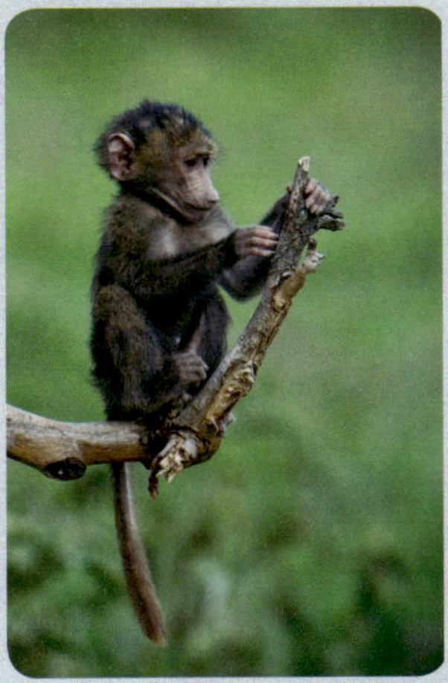

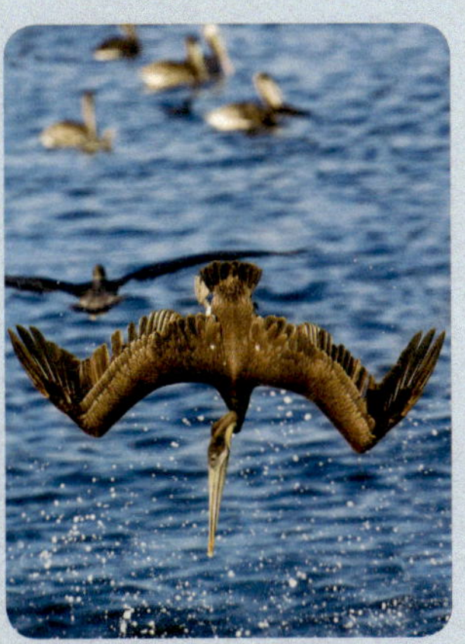

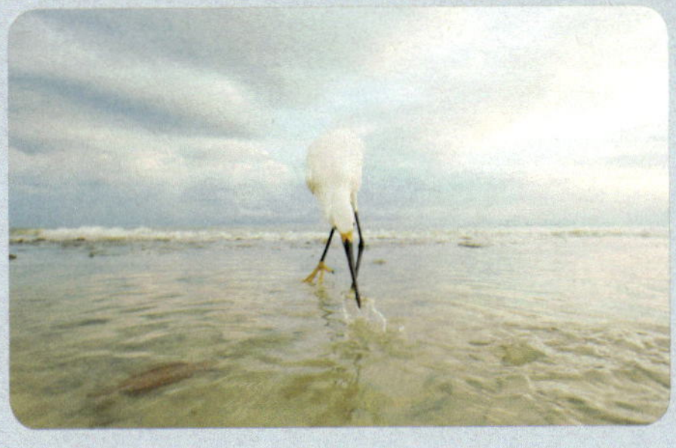

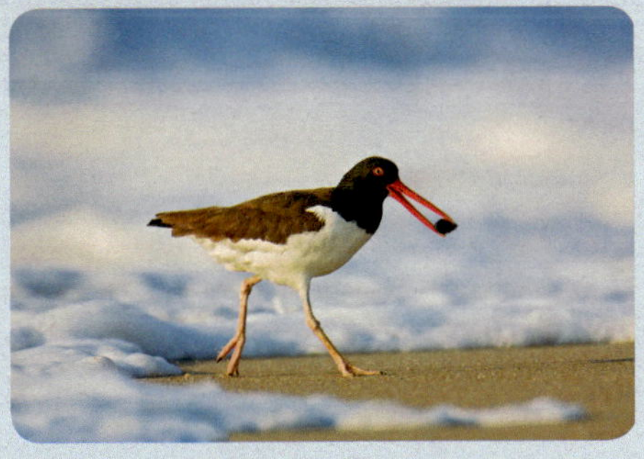

Clockwise from top left:

Emperor Penguin and Iceberg, Snow Hill Island, Antarctica, *©Sue Flood / Tartan Dragon Ltd.*

Young Baboon Deep in Thought, Lake Nakuru, Kenya, *©James Heupel / J. Heupel Photography*

Brown Pelican Dive, Monterey Bay, California, *©Robert Stronck / pixel-gym*

American Oystercatcher, Belmar, New Jersey, *©Jim Gilbert*

Snowy Egret with Fish, Ft. Myers Beach, Florida, *©Adams Serra*

FIND

Clockwise from top left:

Surf Scoter Gathering, Haines, Alaska, *©Judi Rice*

The World Beyond the Den, Colorado, *©Donna Dannen*

Common Terns Discuss the Finer Points of Flight, Tern Restoration Project, White Island, New Hampshire, *©Kevin Klasman*

Bigfin Reef Squid Depositing Eggs, Lembeh Strait, North Sulawesi, Indonesia, *©Christopher Crowley*

Sandhill Cranes, Bosque del Apache National Wildlife Refuge, New Mexico, *©Richard Curtin / Shoreside Images*

DUOS

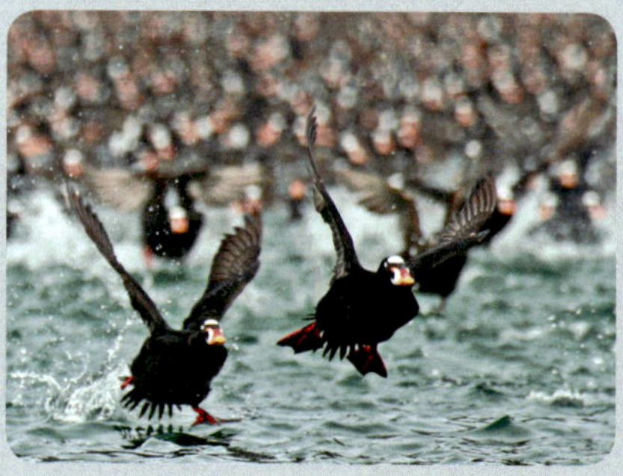

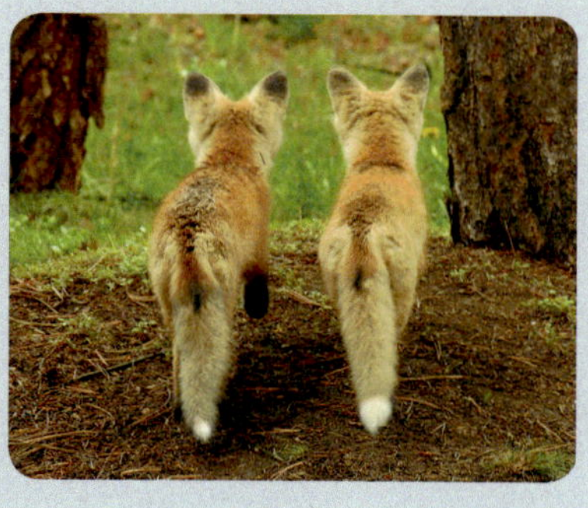

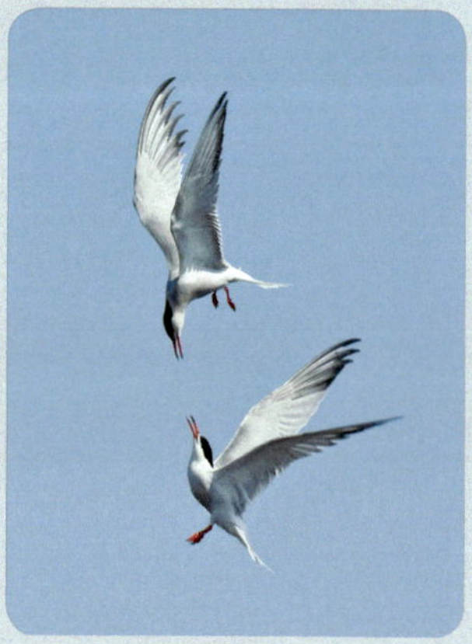

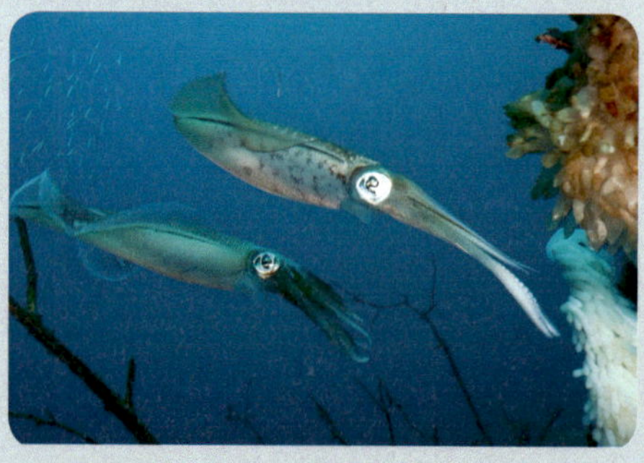

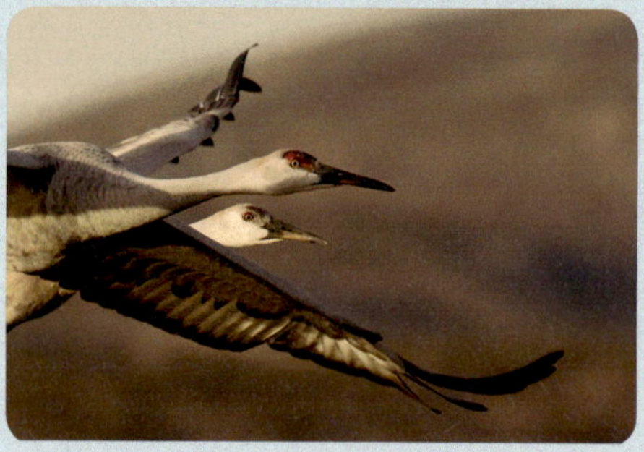

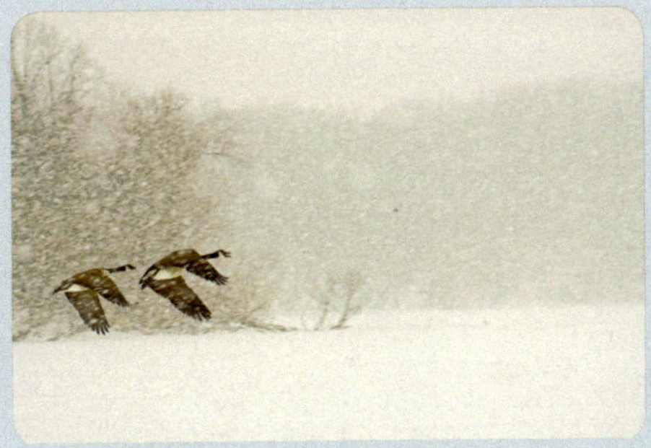

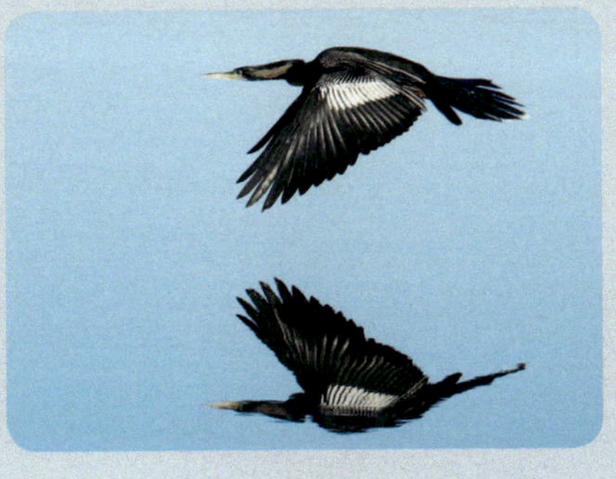

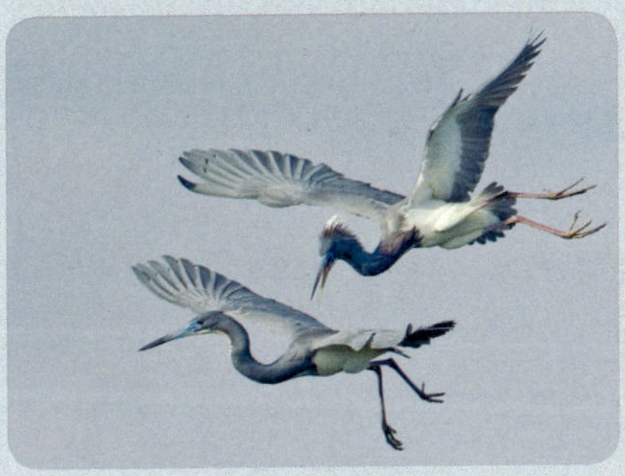

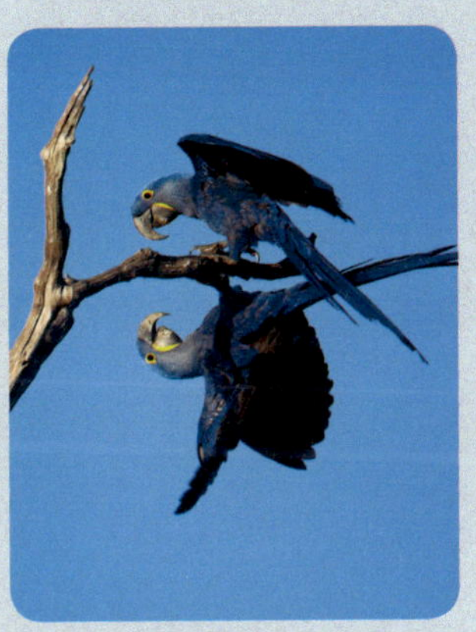

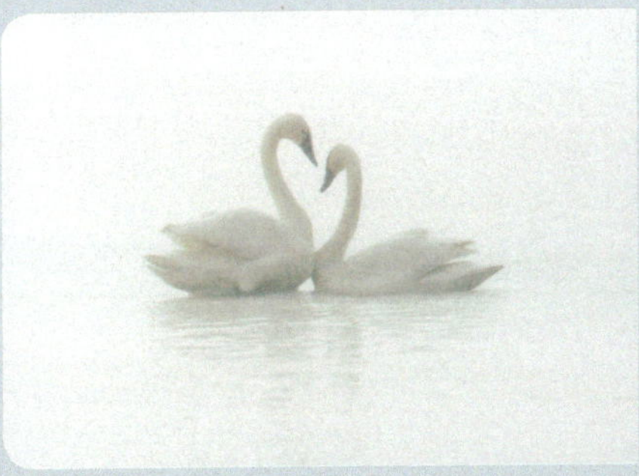

Clockwise from top left:

Canada Geese in Spring Snow, Hottes Lake near Spirit Lake, Iowa, *©Daniel Ruf*

Anhinga Reflected, Wakodahatchee Wetlands, Delray Beach, Florida, *©Michael Rosenbaum*

Hyacinth Macaws, Pantanal, Brazil, *©Cortez Austin / Natural Visions Photography*

Tundra Swans in Fog, Sacramento National Wildlife Refuge, California, *©Susan McConnell*

Tricolor Heron Attack in Breeding Season, Wakodahatchee Wetlands, Delray Beach, Florida, *©Michael Rosenbaum*

DOUBLED

Clockwise from top left:

Not a Survivor, Zion National Park, Utah, *©Jeffrey Sipress / Jeffrey Sipress Photography*

Ospreys Building a Nest, Everglades National Park, Florida, *©Daniel Cedras*

Prickly Pear Cactus at Night, Hidalgo County, Texas, *©Ruth Hoyt / Close To Nature—Images by Ruth Hoyt*

Leopard, Serengeti, Tanzania, *©Bill Harbin*

Marine Iguana on Cliff Wall, Galapagos Islands, Ecuador, *©Greg Lasley*

STICK

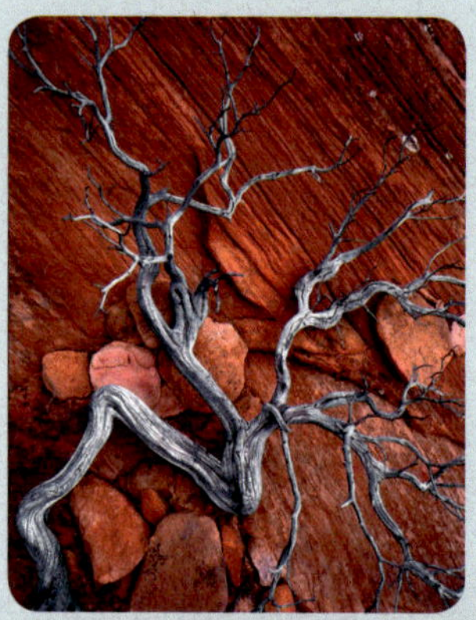
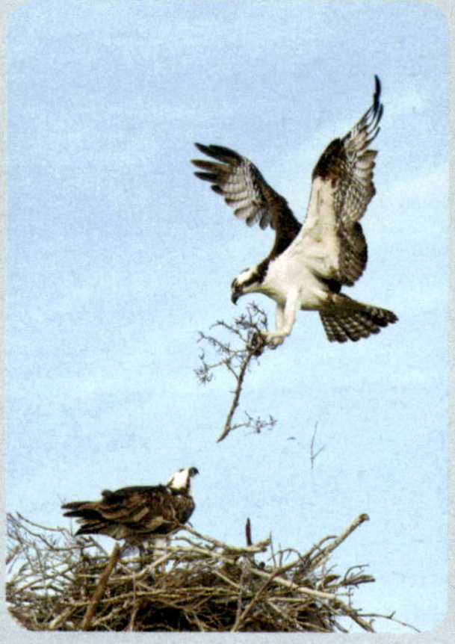
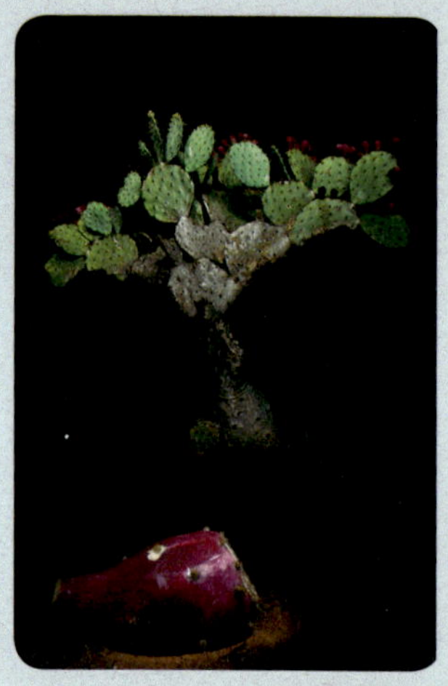
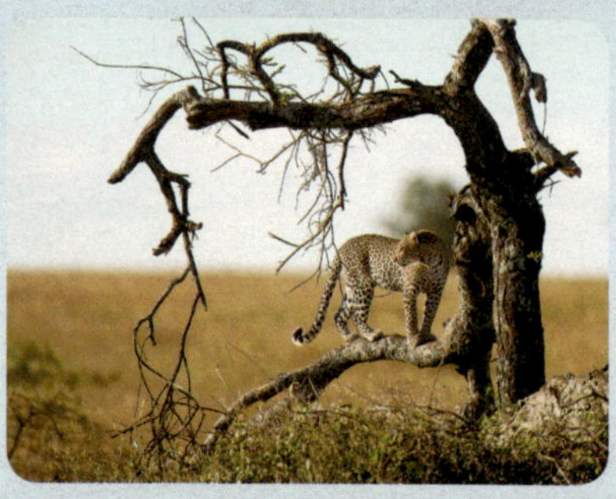
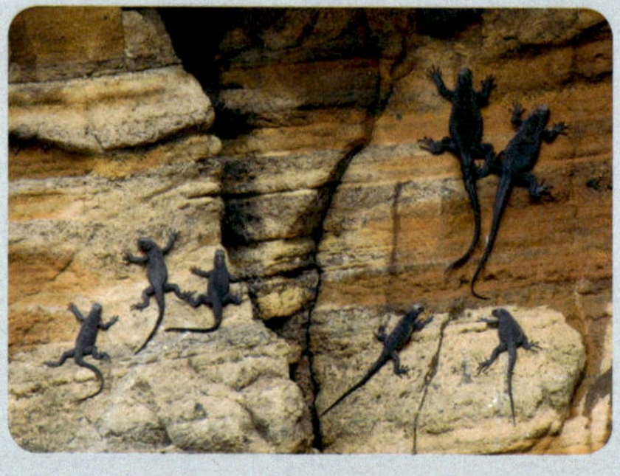

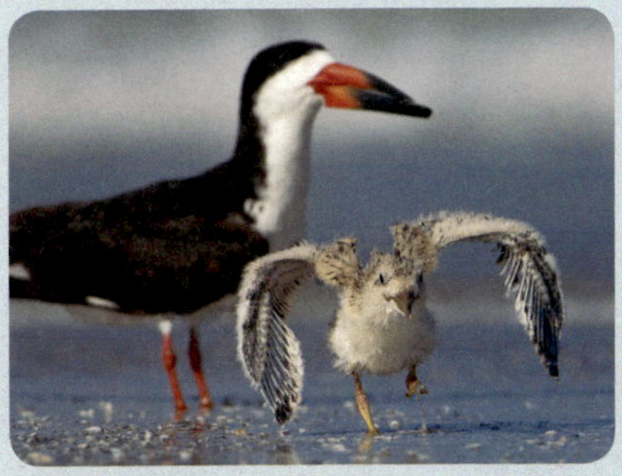

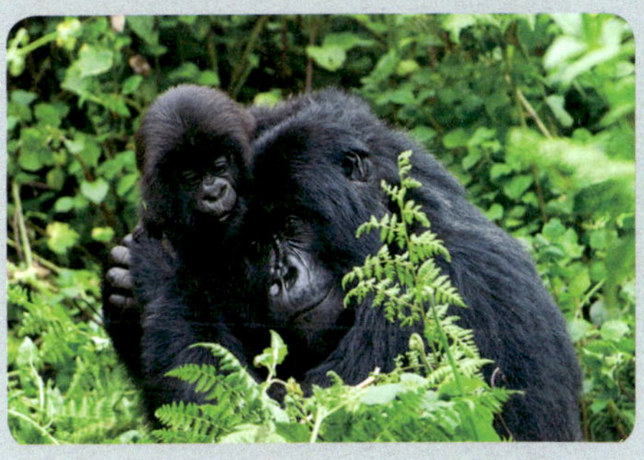

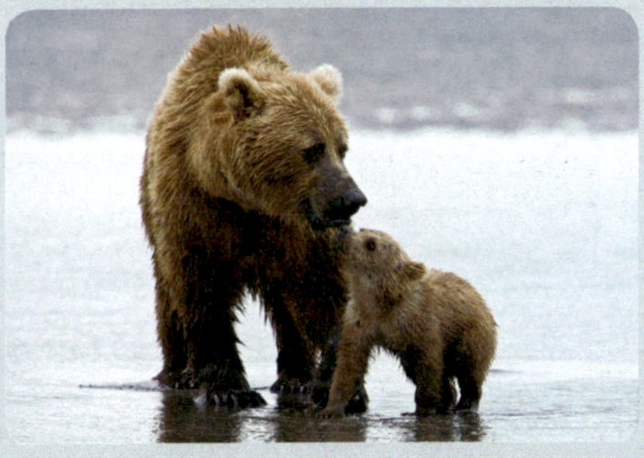

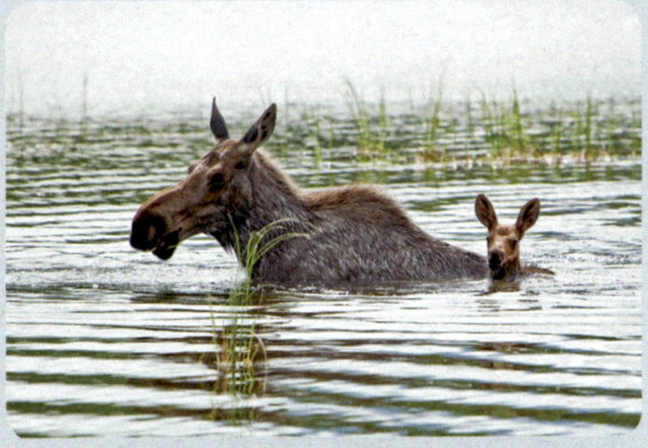

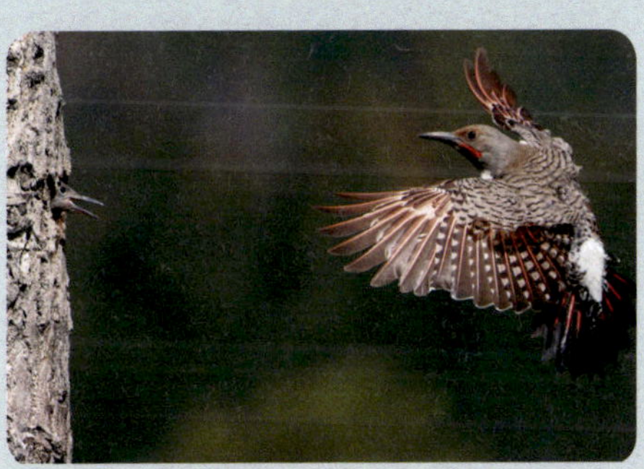

Clockwise from top left:

Black Skimmer Chick—Flight School, Indian Shores, Florida, *©Christina Evans / Chroma-Graphics Studios, Inc.*

Swimming Lessons, Otter Lake, near Anchorage, Alaska, *©Charles Maas / ImagingNorth*

Flicker Approaching Nest Cavity, Rocky Mountain National Park, Colorado, *©Richard Holmes*

Mother and Cub, Lake Clark National Park, Alaska, *©Mac Danzig*

Female Mountain Gorilla Caressing her Young, Volcanoes National Park, Rwanda, *©Dee Ann Pederson / Windows of Nature by Dee Ann*

MATERNAL

Clockwise from top left:

Coquerel's Sifaka Mother and Baby, Anjajavy, northwestern Madagascar, *©Susan McConnell*

Detailing, Sequim, Washington, *©Chris Zink*

Elegant Visitor, Anchorage, Alaska, *©Charles Maas / ImagingNorth*

Fox Kit, Buffalo Bill's Hunting Lodge, Pahaska Tepee, Wyoming, *©Susana Roland*

Blue Dasher Dragonfly, Manhattan, New York City, *©Cynthia Walpole / focus frog, LLC*

SIT

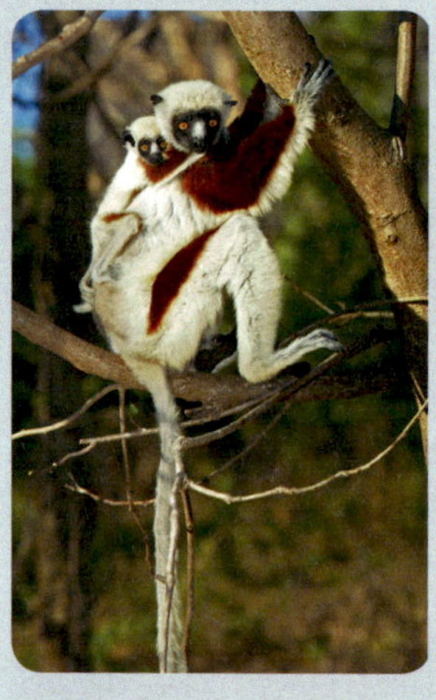

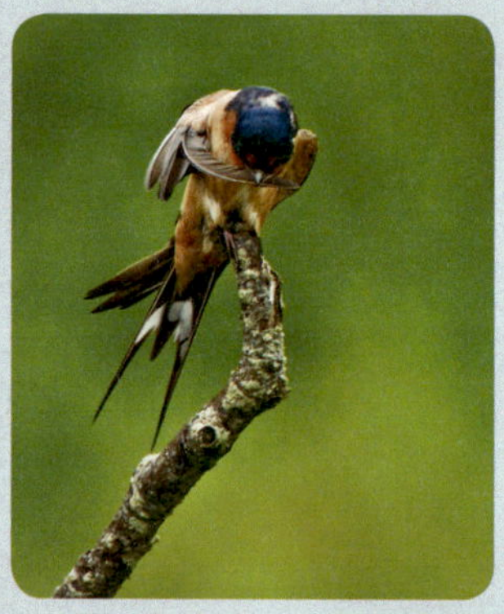

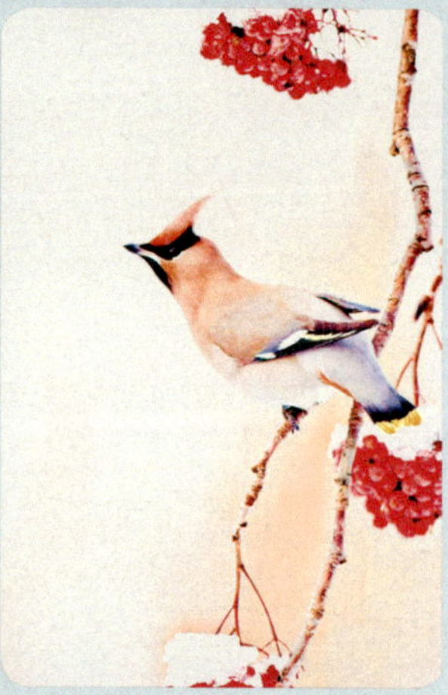

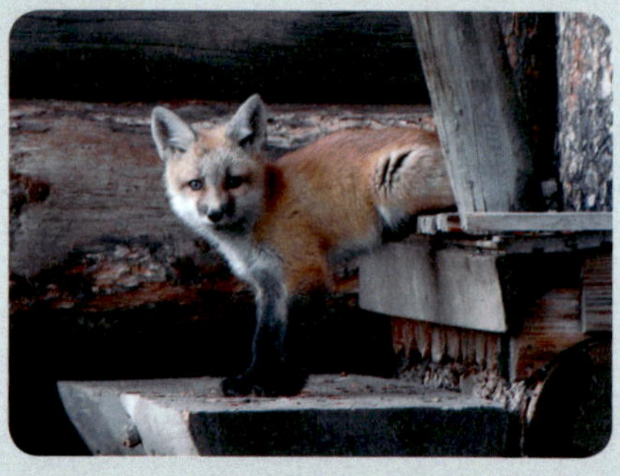

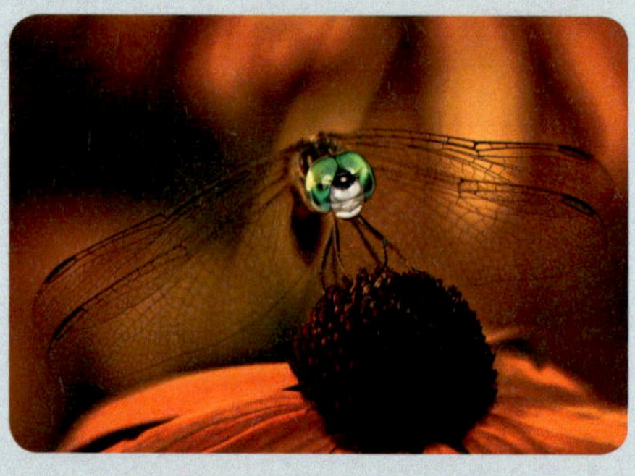

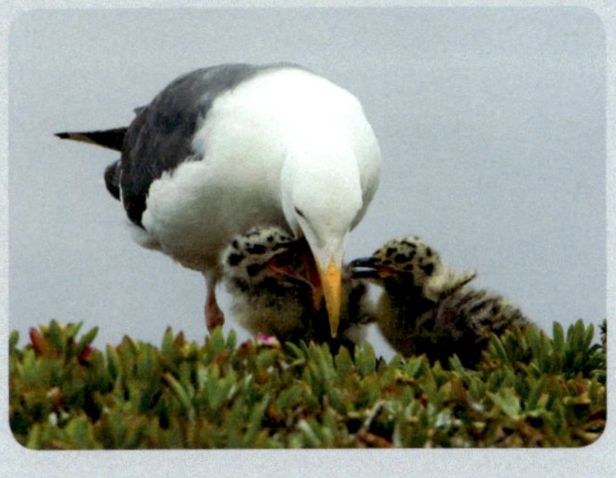

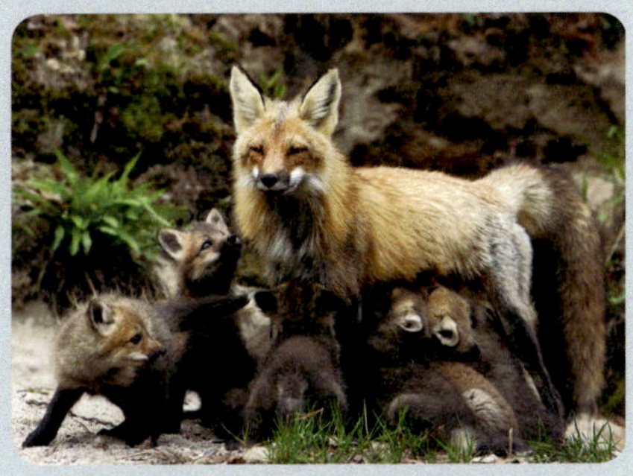

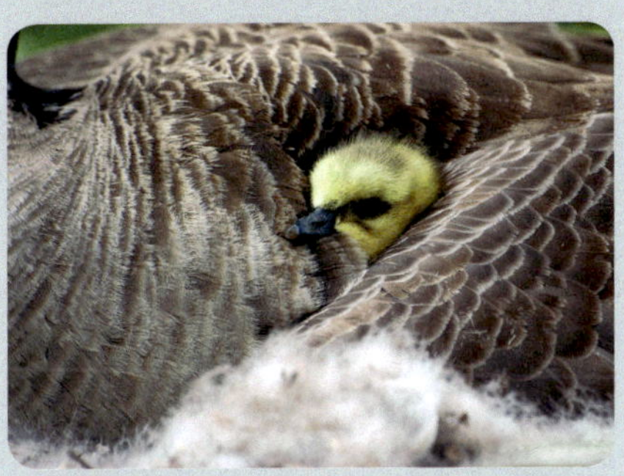

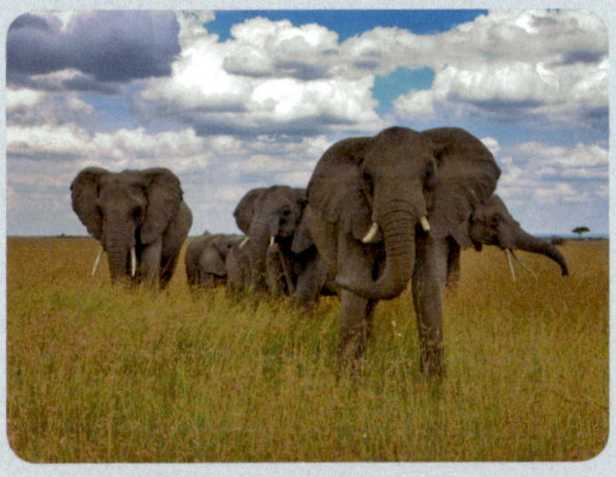

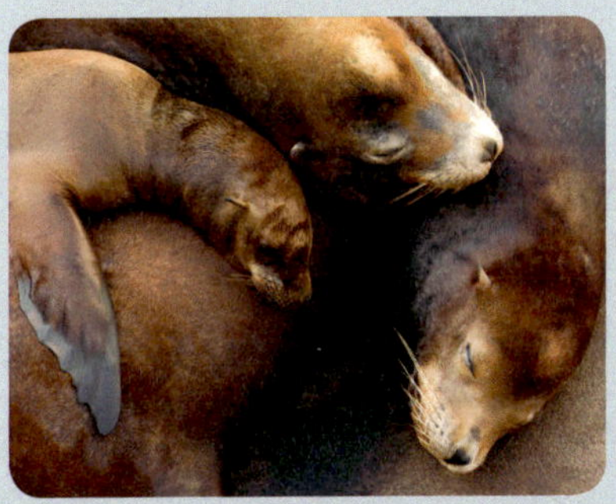

Clockwise from top left:

Herring Gull Feeding Chicks, Fort Bragg, California, *©Brigitte Clough / Captivating Photos by Clough*

Red Fox Pups Feeding Outside Den, Killarney Provincial Park, Ontario, Canada, *©Tamara Caldwell / Enviro-Lynx Photography*

Elephant Herd, Serengeti National Park, Tanzania, *©Chris Gamel*

Sea Lions Sleeping on Dock, Morro Bay, California, *©Teddy Llovet*

Gosling Just after Hatching, Silver Lake, Rochester, Minnesota, *©Deborah Stark*

FAMILY

Contributors

Adams, Ashley, *www.ashleyadamsphoto.com*, ashleyadamsphotography@yahoo.com, 26

Amoruso, Robert / WILDSCAPE IMAGES, *www.wildscapeimages.com*, wildscapeimages@att.net, 28, 60, 70

Austin, Cortez / NATURAL VISIONS PHOTOGRAPHY, *www.cortezaustinphotography.com*, *www.photosourcebook.com/2270*, cortez.austin@verizon.net, 75

Bagshaw, Sean / OUTDOOR EXPOSURE PHOTOGRAPHY, LLC, *www.outdoorexposurephoto.com*, sean@outdoorexposurephoto.com, 26, 36, 42, 60

Barrington, Erwin, e.barrington@comcast.net, 22

Barry, Kevin, *www.agpix.com/kevinbarry*, KBarryPhoto@aol.com, 29, 61

Bauer, Keith, *www.keithbauer.smugmug.com*, kcbauer@juno.com, 40

Becker, David, *www.findingsstudio.com*, dave@fescofire.com, 62

Beisser, Ann, *www.anniebimages.com*, anniebinaz2@aol.com, 56, 59

Beittel, Cliff, *www.agpix.com/cliffbeittel*, cbeittel@aol.com, 63

Block, Bonnie / FIELD AND FARM PHOTOGRAPHY, *www.fieldandfarmphoto.com*, Bonnie@fieldandfarmphoto.com, 30

Bradfield, George / THROUGH NATURE'S EYES PHOTOGRAPHY, *www.thrunatureseyesphotography.com*, georgefbradfield@bellsouth.net, 56

Brauer, Jack / WIDERANGE PHOTO LLC, *www.widerange.org*, jack@widerange.org, 57

Briccetti, Eleanor, *www.briccettiphoto.com*, ebriccetti@comcast.net, 39

Brown, Barry / MISSING PIECES, *www.coralreefphotos.com*, barry@coralreefphotos.com, 27

Brown, Douglas / BIRDWHISPERER PHOTOGRAPHY, *web.me.com/dlb/My_Website/Welcome.html*, dlb@comcast.net, 64

Brown, Jim, info@highplainsreflections.com, 28

Caldwell, Tamara / ENVIRO-LYNX PHOTOGRAPHY, *www.enviro-lynx.com/photography*, enviro-lynx@rogers.com, 79

Campbell, Bill / BILL CAMPBELL PHOTOGRAPHY, *www.billcampbellphoto.com*, bcphoto3@mac.com, 59

Cannon, Kelly, kcannon@yahoo.com, 49

Carr, Donna, *www.DonnaCarrPhotography.com*, donnacarr@comcast.net, 69

Cedras, Daniel, gigophoto@gmail.com, 68, 76

Chappell, Nathan / TROGON TOURS, INC., *www.trogontours.net*, nchappell@trogontours.net, 43, 70

Clough, Brigitte / CAPTIVATING PHOTOS BY CLOUGH, wac2bac98@comcast.net, 79

Coe, Geoff / WILD IMAGES FLORIDA, geoff@wildimagesfla.com, 71

Crowley, Christopher, *www.cjclandandseaphoto.com*, chris.crowley@hughes.net, 33, 67, 74

Curtin, Richard / SHORESIDE IMAGES, Racurtin@hotmail.com, 74

Damron, Nancy, *www.damronphoto.com*, hood1956@satx.rr.com, 34

Dannen, Donna, *www.tundrawinds.zenfolio.com/*, tundrawinds@me.com, 74

Danzig, Mac, *www.macdanzigphotography.com*, macdanzig@yahoo.com, 77

Davis, Harold, *www.photoblog2.com*, info@photoblog2.com, 46

Day, Ron / RON DAY PHOTOGRAPHY, *www.rondayphotography.com*, ronlday@hughes.net, 13, 64

Dayton, Robert, *www.robertdaytonphotography.ifp3.com*, robert.dayton@att.net, 62

DesRochers, David, *www.desrochersphotography.com*, daved199@verizon.net, 61, 69

Domm, Robert / ROBERT DOMM PHOTOGRAPHY, *www.rdommphoto.com*, mail@rdommphoto.com, 38, 39, 54

Duval, Richard / DUVAL IMAGES, rduval@pobox.com, 58

Eaton, Donna / DONNA EATON PHOTOGRAPHY, *www.donnaeatonphoto.com*, deatonphoto@gmail.com, 40

Eberhart, Ronald / RON EBERHART PHOTOGRAPHY, *www.roneberhart.com*, ron@roneberhart.com, 53

Eicher, David / DAVE EICHER PHOTOGRAPHY, *www.eicherfoto.com*, david@eicherfoto.com, 62

Esper, Johnathan / WILDERNESSCAPES PHOTOGRAPHY, *www.wildernessphotographs.com*, johnathanesper@gmail.com, 34

Evans, Christina / CHROMAGRAPHICS STUDIOS, INC., *www.cgstudios.smugmug.com/*, chromagrafx1@tampabay.rr.com, 16, 41, 51, 77

Ferguson, Greg / GREG FERGUSON PHOTOGRAPHY, *www.gregferguson.us.com*, grferguson@comcast.net, 35, 60

Ferguson, Ricky / FOTOS N FINS, *www.fotosnfins.com*, ferguson@txcyber.com, 29, 32, 68

FitzSimmons, David / FITZSIMMONS PHOTOGRAPHY, *www.fitzsimmonsphotography.com*, davefitzsimmons@yahoo.com, 52, 64

Flood, Sue / TARTAN DRAGON LTD, *www.sueflood.com*, sueflood@mac.com, 45, 66, 67, 73

Flynn, Bryce, bryce@bryceflynn-ei.com, 26

Forns, Alfred, *www.Avianscapes.com*, arf2@mac.com, 22, 50, 72

Forns, Fabiola, *www.avianscapes.com*, fabiolad@bellsouth.net, 35, 52

Forseth, Jan / IMAGESOFCOLORADO.COM, *www.imagesofcolorado.com*, janf@imagesofcolorado.com, 16

Friel, Bernard / A DIFFERENT PERSPECTIVE, *www.wampy.com*, wampy@att.net, 31

Galletto, James / JIMMY G'S NATURE PHOTOGRAPHY, *www.jimmygsnaturephotos.homestead.com/jims.html*, tttubes@optonline.net, 9

Gamel, Chris, *www.Animal-Antics.net*, cgamel@satx.rr.com, 63, 79

Gilardini, Daisy, *www.daisygilardini.com*, dgilardini@bluewin.ch, 34, 61, 62, 67

Gilbert, Jim, *www.jimgilbertphoto.com/*, jggilbert@earthlink.net, 17, 69, 73

Glazer, Carol / GLAZER CREATIVE GROUP, glazerphotography@tampabay.rr.com, 44

Glazer, Irwin / GLAZER CREATIVE GROUP, glazbec2@tampabay.rr.com, 17

Goldstein, Sheldon, *www.shellysphotoart.com*, shellyvt1@yahoo.com, 4

Gordon, Jonathan, jmgordon@pol.net, 60

Gozansky, Bill / BILL GOZANSKY PHOTOGRAPHY, *www.billgozansky.com*, info@billgozansky.com, 22, 54

Gray, Chris / SHADES OF GRAY, *www.photogray.ca*, chris@photogray.ca, 40

Grove, Daniel, *www.digitaldragonphoto.com*, dan@digitaldragonphoto.com, 51

Gulick, Amy / AMY GULICK PHOTOGRAPHY, *www.amygulick.com*, info@amygulick.com, 65

Haase, Jude, jude_haase@hotmail.com, 54, 69

Haenchen, Dietmar, haendi@mac.com, 56

Hager, James / JAMES HAGER PHOTOGRAPHY, *www.jameshagerphoto.com*, james@jameshagerphoto.com, 45

Hamburgh, Gary / GARY HAMBURGH PHOTOGRAPHY, *www.garyhamburghphotography.com*, hambga@comcast.net, 21

Hammond, David, *www.davidhammondphotography.com*, infocus4@verizon.net, 60

Haney, Chuck / CHUCK HANEY OUTDOOR PHOTOGRAPHY, *www.chuckhaney.com*, chuck@chuckhaney.com, 48

Harbin, Bill, wpharb@comcast.net, 30, 59, 76

Hardesty, Lara / LARA HARDESTY NATURE IMAGES, lahardesty@comcast.net, 21

Hart, Jay, jayrhart@comcast.net, 58

Hart, Kim / KIM HART WILDLIFE PHOTOGRAPHY, *www.khartwildphoto.com*, kim@khartwildphoto.com, 19

Heine, Gero / GERO HEINE PHOTOGRAPHY, *www.geroheine.com*, gero@geroheine.com, 67

Henry, Michael, henry.michael@mayo.edu, 50, 71

Hershberger, Wil / NATURE IMAGES AND SOUNDS, *www.natureimagesandsounds.com*, wil@natureimagesandsounds.com, 38

Heupel, James / J HEUPEL PHOTOGRAPHY, *www.jheupelphotography.com*, jheupelphotography@gmail.com, 73